century, Sicilian gangs brought the extortion tactics they practiced
ork. Out of these Mano Nera—Black Hand gangs—the first Sicilian
inal organization in America, Cosa Nostra, was formed.

In the late 1.
at home to Neu
cr

The Don:
36 Rules of the Bosses

RJ Roger

A Joost Elffers Book

CITADEL PRESS
Kensington Publishing Corp.
kensingtonbooks.com

To my father and mother, Roger and Beverley Rudolph.

CONTENTS

The Family Structure   10

Prologue: The Origins of Cosa Nostra   18

The Five Epochs of the Bosses

Epoch 1:   Cooking Pot   50

Epoch 2:   Made   62

Epoch 3:   Boss   74

Epoch 4:   Red Pepper   86

Epoch 5:   Rosebush   98

Interlude: The Bosses and Machiavelli   106

The 36 Rules of the Bosses

Rule 1:   Use a Skilled Man to Your Benefit   111

Rule 2:   Beware of the Kiss   115

Rule 3:   Step Down, Retire   119

Rule 4:   Kiss the Ring   123

Rule 5:   Mix with the Soldiers   129

Rule 6:   Invest Totally   133

Rule 7:   Be Vigilant of Your Rivals   137

Rule 8:   Break the Rules   141

Rule 9:   Dress Dapper   145

Rule 10:   Kill the Boss   149

Rule 11:   Accept Risk   155

Rule 12:   Align with High Rank   159

Rule 13:   Say Nothing   163

Rule 14:   Impose Harsh Rules   169

Rule 15:   Avoid Routine   175

Rule 16:   Keep a Stash   179

Rule 17:   Loyalty Is a Lie   183

Rule 18:   Pay Your Soldiers Well   187

Rule 19:   Speak the Language of a Soldier   191

Rule 20:   Take It to the Mattress   195

Rule 21:   Be Honorable   199

Rule 22:   Take Your Bullet   203

Rule 23:   Keep Your Hands Clean   207

Rule 24:   Every Man Has a Price   211

Rule 25:   Take What's Yours   217

Rule 26:   Honor the Boss   221

Rule 27:   The End Justifies the Means   225

Rule 28:   Build Relationships   229

Rule 29:   Respect Your Public   233

Rule 30:   Start Early   237

Rule 31:   Control the Purse   243

Rule 32:   Bosses Talk to Bosses   247

Rule 33:   Do a Favor for a Favor   251

Rule 34:   Live Modestly   255

Rule 35:   Be Informed   259

Rule 36:   Buy a Plot   263

Acknowledgments   269

THE FAMILY
STRUCTURE

BOSS

CONSIGLIERE

UNDERBOSS

CAPO REGIME

CAPO REGIME

CAPO REGIME

SOLDIERS

SOLDIERS

SOLDIERS

A S S O C I A T E S

FAMILY

1

An underworld organization.

2

A profit-driven enterprise or business.

BOSS OF BOSSES

1

The leader of every Cosa Nostra Family in the United States. The man to whom every boss in the country reports.

2

The topmost Cosa Nostra rank ever to exist
in the United States.

3

Sometimes referred to as the capo di tutti capi.

BOSS

1

A leader of a Cosa Nostra Family.

2

Sometimes referred to as a capo, godfather, father, or don.

UNDERBOSS

1

The topmost aide to the boss. The second-in-command
and second-most-powerful position within a Family.

2

Sometimes referred to as a sottocapo.

CONSIGLIERE

1
The third-in-command within a Family.
An adviser to the boss.

2
A human-resources officer for the soldiers,
resolving disputes between soldiers and caporegimes.

CAPOREGIME

1
An executive within a Family.

2
The leader of a crew/regime of soldiers.

3
Sometimes referred to as a skipper,
captain, capo, or capodecine.

SOLDIER

1
A subordinate to a caporegime.

2
The bottommost rank within a Family, assigned
to one who has no authority. An entry-level rank.

3
A member of a crew/regime.

4
Sometimes referred to as a made guy,
wiseguy, or "friend of ours."

ASSOCIATE

1
A nonmember affiliate of a Cosa Nostra
member who participates in crimes or schemes associated with the
Family.

2
An apprentice working for a soldier or
caporegime to prove himself worthy of membership.

3
A man sometimes considered "on record"
with a member, meaning that the member is
considered responsible for all activities and
actions committed by the associate.

CREW
A group of soldiers working at the behest
of a caporegime. Sometimes referred
to as a regime or decine.

In 1963, Joseph Valachi became the first member of Cosa Nostra to break his oath of omertà. In congressional hearings that would become famous as the Valachi Hearings, he revealed the inner workings of the organization to Senator John McClellan's Senate Investigations Committee. Valachi testified that he wanted to destroy the leaders of Cosa Nostra because they had long mistreated the lower-level members. The following passage from his testimony is the reason I write this book in his honor.

CHAIRMAN

Would you tell us why you decided to cooperate
with the Department of Justice and its agencies
and with this committee?

JOE VALACHI

The main answer to that is very simple:
it is to destroy them.

CHAIRMAN

Destroy who?

JOE VALACHI

The Cosa Nostra leaders; the bosses.

CHAIRMAN

You want to destroy the whole syndicate?

JOE VALACHI

That is right. Yes, sir.

CHAIRMAN

Why do you feel like it should be destroyed?

JOE VALACHI

They have been very bad to the soldiers and they have been thinking for themselves all through the years.

PROLOGUE:
THE ORIGINS
OF COSA NOSTRA

Cosa Nostra is a secret society. Its exact date of origin is unknown, but its central structure, ideals, and rituals can be traced to the Sicily of the mid-1800s and it migrated to the United States later in that century. At the height of its power, in the 1950s, Cosa Nostra —"this thing of ours"— operated in every major city in the country, controlling politicians, lawmen, and all aspects of commerce. It had billions of dollars in annual revenues. Its power was far reaching—as high as the US president and cabinet.

The Cosa Nostra of that period had about thirty Families—individual criminal organizations led by a single boss. The most powerful group, known as the "Five Families," worked out of New York City. The heads of the Five Families, known as the Bosses, made up the Commission. Because they did not abide by the rules of outside governments or systems of order, these five bosses recognized themselves as a sovereign state.

To be a member of Cosa Nostra you must be pure-blooded Italian, you must be male, and you must swear the blood oath of omertà— an oath of silence, promising not to reveal the society's secrets or even its existence—before a member of an administration. An administration is a hierarchy within a Family consisting of a boss, an underboss, and a consigliere. The penalty for breaking the oath of omertà is death. Cosa Nostra is a secret society to such a degree that its codes call for it to be viewed as nonexistent. *The Don: 36 Rules of the Bosses* codifies its doctrine. This is the most revealing account of Cosa Nostra society ever drafted.

To understand Cosa Nostra, you must first understand where and when it was established: in nineteenth-century Sicily. The Italian writer Luigi Barzini Jr. wrote in 1972, "The reason why Sicily is ungovernable is that the inhabitants have long ago learned to distrust and neutralize all written laws and to govern themselves in their own rough, homemade fashion, as if official institutions did not exist. This arrangement is highly unsatisfactory because it cures no ills, promotes injustice and tyranny, leaves crimes unpunished, does not make use of the Sicilians' best qualities, and has kept the country stagnant and backward in almost every way." Barzini accurately describes what drove Sicilians from their homeland to the United States at the turn of the last century—about 4 million between the 1880s and the early 1920s, all dreaming of a better life. The island was ungoverned and in ruin, hijacked by its own inhabitants to enrich the upper few at the expense of the lower many.

What empowered those upper few was the lower many's long-held distrust of outsiders and of the institution of government. Sicilians had defended their land from invaders for many centuries. In 1860, though, the island was finally, forcibly annexed by Giuseppe Garibaldi as he worked to consolidate what would become the Kingdom of Italy. The new government seized Sicilian land and redistributed it among the peasantry, anticipating that it would be cultivated and an economy would be established. The peasantry made good use of this gift; for the first time they owned land that they could nurture and call their own. They farmed and traded what they grew, developing vineyards and lemon groves for modest profits. But they quickly learned that even under the rule of a strong Italian government, their problems would remain: the more they prospered, the more they had to fend off bandits and extortionists. They had no protection. Their only way to maintain their property was to negotiate with the thieves who routinely preyed on them.

The people were angry and their lives were hard, but they distrusted the Italian government more than their local brethren. To Sicilians, the Italians were just another group of invaders hijacking their land. About their homegrown predators, on the other hand, many felt, "They are bad people, but they are our bad people."

Foreign invaders—Greek, French, Arab, Norman, Spanish—had long terrorized Sicily. A common teaching among Sicilians is that to truly know someone, you have to know the three fathers preceding them. If you don't know the fathers three generations back, don't trust them. In a tale widely circulated among Sicilians, a French soldier violently raped a Palermo woman on her wedding day. Her mother, seeing her daughter assaulted, ran for help, loudly shouting in the street, "*Ma fia, ma fia*," "My daughter, my daughter"—hence the word "mafia," popularly used to describe bandits and outlaws. Such stories constantly remind Sicilians to be suspicious of outsiders. Italian rule only intensified their distrust. Under annexation, Sicily's economy remained poor, political corruption worsened, and wealth and power became more concentrated, resting firmly in the hands of an organized group who constituted an illegitimate government. In his 1864 report *Pubblica sicurezza in Sicilia* (Public safety in Sicily), the politician Niccolò Turrisi Colonna, twice mayor of Palermo and the survivor of an assassination attempt in 1863, described this group as a "sect of thieves that has ties across the whole island."

Turrisi's "sect of thieves" took orders from local "men of honor" who were members of the "Honored Society." Besides leading criminals, these men of honor acted as moderators, peacekeepers of sorts, resolving disputes and brokering deals without involving police or judges. They oversaw small boroughs and communities in Sicily. And they themselves took orders from a smaller group of powerful men who controlled larger territories and had political contacts in Palermo and Rome.

Sicilian peasants bartered with each other to gain access to goods and services that they needed. They had no political resources and they feared going outside the underground network for support—the outlaws were increasingly organized and politically connected and to cross them could lead to death. Annexation had only empowered the Honored Society, which was now able to seize investments pouring into Sicily from Rome. This shadow group became known as Cosa Nostra.

The society established membership rituals, notably the blood oath of loyalty for new members: a knife was used to prick the man's trigger finger, drawing blood that was then smeared from the fingertip onto an image of a saint. After blood was wiped over the image, it was burned, symbolizing the new member's burning soul if he were ever to betray the organization. This ritual began sometime in the mid-1850s, though exactly when and where is unknown. It was first made public in 1875, by a police chief in Palermo.

By 1880, Cosa Nostra had monopolized power throughout Sicily. The Italian government could not and did not try to loosen its grip on the populace. The group was so strong that even Niccolò Colonna—that is, even the mayor of Palermo, as Colonna was in 1881–82 and again in 1886–87—is believed to have become an associate or perhaps a full member of the organization. Once staunchly opposed to the "sect of thieves that has ties across the whole island," he may even have become the head of Cosa Nostra—or so thought Domenico Farini, president of the Italian senate from 1887 until almost the end of the century.

Under Cosa Nostra rule, Sicily was at best stagnant, at worst, and more convincingly, regressive. The economy worsened, education was poor, medical care was hard to come by and reserved for the well-to-do, and the only available work was labor-intensive for minimal pay. Rank-and-file Sicilians lived in dire conditions, and the little they had was taxed by the island's shadow government. With no apparent end in sight, Sicilians began to flee to America.

In the spring of 1901, J. P. Morgan formed U.S. Steel. It grew to be the largest corporation in the world—the first billion-dollar corporation. But according to the renowned Jewish gangster Meyer Lansky, Cosa Nostra was bigger. In

Francis Ford Coppola's 1974 film *The Godfather II*, the gangster character Hyman Roth states, "We're bigger than U.S. Steel." The remark is believed to quote Lansky.

Don Giuseppe Bonanno was a powerful mafioso in the nineteenth-century Sicilian Cosa Nostra. He was an uncle of Joseph Bonanno, later the longest-serving boss of the Five Families in New York. A product of Sicily, Don Giuseppe schooled his underlings in the most sacred of all Cosa Nostra rules: *say nothing*. According to Bill Bonanno, son of Joe Bonanno, one day, without explanation, Don Giuseppe summoned a soldier to a meeting. The soldier arrived. Don Giuseppe told him to take off his shirt, kneel, and stay still and silent. The soldier complied. Unbeknownst to him, though, Don Giuseppe was not disciplining but teaching.

Don Giuseppe picked up a plaited bullwhip and began to whip the soldier's back until it was welted and bloodied. As ordered, the soldier took the beating in silence. Afterward, Don Giuseppe told him to go clean himself, treat his wounds, get dressed, and then come back. The soldier again did as instructed, treating his wounds with lemon juice to prevent infection. When he returned, Don Giuseppe was removing his own jacket and shirt. He went up to the soldier: "Take the whip and give me twice as many lashes as I gave you. Mind you, if you don't whip me as hard as I whipped you, I'll give you a second beating."

Though frightened, the soldier proceeded to whip Don Giuseppe, marking his back with welts. Don Giuseppe took the beating stoically. Once done, the soldier stepped back, unsure what to expect. But Don Giuseppe told him, "Do you understand how it is? It's one thing to say you're never going to talk against your friends, but it's quite another not to talk when someone beats you. I wanted to see how well you took a beating."

The soldier understood the lesson: Cosa Nostra is a secret society protected by its oath of omertà, its code of silence. This was the principle that enabled it to cross the Atlantic to the United States and grow to be "bigger than U.S. Steel."

It was the early 1880s. Fleeing political turbulence, disease, natural disaster, social disorder, and poverty, the first large wave of Sicilians began to emigrate to America. Many were unaffiliated with Cosa Nostra but some were members, sent to America by their bosses with instructions to plant the society's roots in the land of opportunity.

They settled first in New Orleans and later in New York, throughout Brooklyn, the Bronx, and most famously Lower Manhattan, where the largest concentration of Italians was in the neighborhood around Mulberry Street eventually recognized as "Little Italy." In America, Sicilians preserved cultural habits developed in their homeland, grouping in close-quartered communities with values of family, food, ethnic purity, and distrust of the state and of outsiders, and with hierarchies of order that had been norms in Sicily for hundreds of years.

Yet America was a difficult transition. Most Sicilians worked in harsh and unsanitary conditions. Further, they were among the lowest-paid workers in the country. Xenophobia was widespread, and Sicilians were ridiculed for their cultural differences and blamed for taking American jobs—even though the United States was experiencing a labor shortage and desperately needed unskilled labor. To help their families survive, young children ditched school and went to work in factories, mines, and farms, or sold newspapers on city streets.

In 1891, a New Orleans police chief was shot and killed. "Sicilian gangsters" were blamed. Nineteen Italians were arrested, charged, and found innocent, but shortly after their acquittal they were kidnapped from the police station and lynched. Sicilians were stereotyped as violent, criminal peasants. They were "treated worse than dogshit," Frank Costello, boss of the Luciano Family, told actor and friend, Gianni Russo. "I want to explain something to you," he went on, producing an ad from the *New York Times*:

> You see this here? . . . I've had it since the day it came out. Here, read it. That ad is over forty years old, and I kept it because I looked into that when I was young—younger than you. That job paid Italians less than anyone else on the site, and it pissed me off. The point I'm trying to make here is Italians were treated worse than dogshit when most of the immigrants came over. A lot of that prejudice still lingers today. *This thing of ours* was started as a matter of survival—to be able to compete. My point is, what we do isn't all about money. It's about equality, respect, and power. Never lose sight of that as you get older and become more involved in what we do.

When Italians began to establish themselves in New York, the city's police force was largely Irish. These cops were skeptical of Italians and left them to fend for themselves. Much as in Sicily, Italian communities throughout New York's five boroughs became domiciles governed by their own. Disputes, protection, and policing were handled internally by leaders of small street gangs. These gangs—five or six young Sicilians acculturated under the teaching of their homeland—would later begin to connect and group, consolidating power, wealth, and territory and laying the foundation for the development of the American Cosa Nostra. Through threats of violence and promises of protection or economic benefit, small gangs were absorbed or swallowed up by larger ones of increasing strength.

The first major Cosa Nostra boss in New York was Giuseppe "Clutch Hand" Morello. His nickname derived from a birth defect: his right hand had only a pinky finger and resembled a claw.

Morello was born in Corleone, Sicily. His father, Calogero Morello, died when he was very young, and his mother, Angelina Piazza, remarried a high-ranking and respected member of the Sicilian Cosa Nostra, Bernardo Terranova, a member of the Corleonesi Family. By this second marriage she had four children: Nick, Ciro, Vincent, and their sister Salvatrice. Terranova proposed his three sons and stepson, Giuseppe Morello, for membership in the Corleonesi Family. They became enforcers, carrying out beatings and murders for the boss.

The town of Corleone hosted a private police force, the Guardie Campestri, which was tasked with combating Cosa Nostra. The head of this force was a man called Giovanni Vella. Unlike the American members of Cosa Nostra, the Sicilians did not consider outsiders off limits: anyone who got in their way—women, children, judges, media, law enforcement—could be killed. This made them powerful: since any opposition was subject to retribution, no one dared to challenge them.

Morello was ordered to kill Vella. He succeeded—Vella died—but the hit was sloppy: Morello was immediately arrested, the murder weapon was found, and an eyewitness, Anna DiPuma, was questioned by police.

Cosa Nostra forces went to work to keep Morello from being convicted. Shortly after his arrest, the murder weapon went missing from police storage and DiPuma was shot and killed. With neither evidence nor witness, the police had to let Morello go. After his release, he fled to New York.

In the United States, Morello would quickly become one of the most feared and ruthless criminals in the country. Forming a gang called the 107th Street Gang, he introduced extortion tactics popular in Sicily to prey on fellow Italians, coming to own stores, bars, restaurants, and real estate and running a large counterfeiting operation. Morello was connected in both New Orleans and New York, America's two major Italian hubs. In 1898, he merged the 107th Street Gang with a gang run by his brother-in-law, Ignazio "Lupo the Wolf" Saietta, the husband of his half-sister, Salvatrice Terranova. Saietta's gang used the *Mano Nera*— "Black Hand"—extortion tactics practiced by a number of criminal groups: a handwritten letter carrying a black handprint was placed in the mailbox of a business or affluent home, or sent there by US mail. The letter demanded cash in exchange for safety and a promise that the money would be repaid in "other ways" that went undefined.

Black Hand gangsters made good on their threats. Those who refused to comply had their homes or businesses firebombed and their children or other loved ones abducted or killed. In the winter of 1905, a Black Hander sent a letter to a New York businessman:

> Esteemed friend: Knowing that you are of a philanthropic turn of mind and of a generous disposition, we wish you to know that we are in need of money—in fact, in dire circumstances. We are therefore forced to ask you for one thousand dollars and in receiving this amount we will be forever grateful, and will repay you in other ways many times over. You will deliver this small amount to a man wearing a red bandana handkerchief on his right arm. He will first ask you for a match. You are to go to the end of the Third Avenue surface line at 59th street, South Brooklyn; thence you will walk along the road leading to Coney Island until our brother meets you. To him you will deliver the money in a small bag without uttering one word. Come alone, for six of us will be stationed along the road. Unless you comply with this request, we will blow up your establishment with dynamite, so you see we mean business.

The businessman didn't take the letter seriously and threw it away. Eleven days later he received a second one:

> We see that you have not complied with our request of a few days ago. You must not think that you are dealing with an ordinary class of men, for we are desperate and fearless. We again ask you to deliver the money at the appointed place on Monday, 11 pm. Don't fail to be there, and come alone, for we shall not tolerate another delay. Before we only threatened to destroy your house. Now both you and your wife will be blown into eternity if you do not obey this friendly letter.

Again the man did not comply, but now he was scared. He saw that the threat was real and was unsure what to do: he did not have the money, he was afraid to contact the police, his wife was ill, and he had a newborn child. He decided to leave town to ask a friend for help. The gang was watching his house and business and knew that he had left, so they sent a third letter, this time to his ailing wife:

> Friend Madam: We are sorry to have to disturb you, but your husband does not seem to take us seriously; but by the blood of the Madonna we will strike soon. Does he think that we are joking with him that he thus wastes our time? We shall give him one more chance and then if you do not advise him to obey us—the vendetta! Let him come to the same meeting place and all will yet be well. If he does not do so, the Madonna protect him and you, for it will mean the death of you both.

The businessman eventually decided to contact the authorities. In this rare case, he and his wife and child, and his home and business, were left unharmed—but the family lived in fear for years to come.

The Black Hand gangs were the darkest element of the Italian immigration wave. A new reality for Americans to reckon with, their brutality fueled the xenophobia that many already felt toward Italians. The American Cosa Nostra grew out of such groups. Morello's partnership with Saietta's Black Hand group, which was based on Mott Street in Little Italy, is recognized by historians as the first major organized criminal Sicilian organization in New York. With the help of his three half-brothers, Ciro, Nick, and Vincent, and with Lupo the Wolf serving as his number two, Morello was now the most powerful man in the growing Sicilian underworld. Today he is recognized as the first capo di tutti capi, the first boss of bosses, in America.

By 1910, though, both Morello and Saietta were behind bars, convicted of counterfeiting. They tried to control their operation from prison but their Family splintered and their power waned. Morello's brother Nick Terranova held on to what was left of the organization and tried to keep the clan intact, but Salvatore "Toto" D'Aquila, leader of a crew within the Morello gang that controlled East Harlem, broke away as an independent gang leader, free of Morello and Saietta. What remained of the Morello faction is known today as the Genovese Family, the oldest of the Five Families in New York. The D'Aquila clan is now known as the Gambino Family.

With Morello and Saietta in jail, D'Aquila grew in power and is recognized by historians as the second boss of bosses in the United States. He expanded his operation into Brooklyn and Lower Manhattan and mentored two of the underworld's future leaders, Manfredi Mineo and Frank Scalise.

In 1920, Morello left prison and tried to retake control of his operations in New York, but D'Aquila immediately ordered his killing. To strengthen and protect himself, Morello aligned with Giuseppe "Joe the Boss" Masseria, who, like D'Aquila, had at one time worked for him. Most of Morello's organization was now unified under Masseria. Understanding that his power had waned, Morello brokered a deal with Masseria that gave him a second-in-command role. He was still respected in Sicily and was feared all over New York. Masseria for his part knew that he could use Morello to help usurp power from D'Aquila.

Indeed, though D'Aquila's rule remained unmatched for the next eight years, Masseria had established himself and his gang grew in power. And in October 1928, on Masseria's orders, Mineo, D'Aquila's most trusted ally, betrayed his boss and organized the killing of D'Aquila, who was shot dead on Avenue A in Manhattan. Mineo seized control of the D'Aquila gang and brought it under Masseria's umbrella. Masseria now was boss of bosses in America.

The last major hurdle standing in the way of Joe Masseria was the Castellammarese clan in Brooklyn, headed by Salvatore Maranzano. Masseria and Maranzano were the heads of the two largest Cosa Nostra groups in the country—and only one of them could be number one, the capo di tutti capi.

On top of that, Masseria and Maranzano hated each other. Their feud would not end until one of them was dead. Masseria was tough and had more soldiers, more guns, more money, and control over a larger territory; Maranzano was rising in power and had support from Don Vito Cascio Ferro, one of the most powerful bosses in Sicily. Maranzano was also smart and strategic and had patience and foresight. Having studied in a seminary to become a priest, he was formally educated and well read. He is said to have spoken many languages; the exact number is debated.

Maranzano was born in the small Sicilian town of Castellammare del Golfo in 1886. As a member of the Magaddino Family, serving under boss Stefano Magaddino, he grew up with the original ideals of the Sicilian Cosa Nostra. He made his bones fighting against the rival Buccellato

Family. When Maranzano left Sicily for the United States, in or around 1918, he was one of the most respected men in the Sicilian underworld.

When Maranzano arrived in New York, he was welcomed into the Castellammarese clan in Brooklyn. He was a skilled entrepreneur, using his profits from a legitimate real estate business and illegitimate bootlegging to establish himself as a financier for schemes both legal and illegal. Nicknamed "Little Caesar" for his admiration of Julius Caesar, according to author Martin Gosch, Maranzano proposed for the American Cosa Nostra a strict order modeled on that of Caesar's legions. The Roman *legionarii* had been indoctrinated into loyalty and obedience. Additionally, like Cosa Nostra, the legions had divisions and subdivisions: the cohort, of about 500 men (the numbers varied over Rome's history); the *centuria*, of 60 to 100 men, led by a centurion; and the *contubernium*, of 8 to 10 men, led by a *decanus*. This structure enforced a strict chain of command, with all loyalties granted to one's direct superior. Though accounts of this history vary, according to Gosch this was the ideal by which Maranzano reorganized Cosa Nostra.

Maranzano's most trusted soldier was Joe Bonanno, future boss of the Bonanno Family. Maranzano, a religious zealot, mentored Bonanno both before and after the first war within the American Cosa Nostra, the Castellammarese War of 1930–31. In return, he became Bonanno's first hero. The younger man would later write,

> Maranzano was handsome. He could make his face smile sweetly, or he could look severe enough to make you tremble. He liked fine clothes. He dressed like a conservative businessman, preferring gray or blue suits, soft pinstripes on the blues. He didn't wear any jewelry other than a watch and his wedding band....
>
> He had a sweet voice, not at all gruff or basso profundo. His voice had an entrancing echolike quality. When Maranzano used his

voice assertively, to give a command, he was the bellknocker and you were the bell.

Maranzano could make everyone in a crowded room think he was talking to him individually. He tailored his speeches to the mentality of his audience. To a simple audience, he spoke in parables; to a more intelligent audience he proclaimed ideas. He knew how to interlace a speech with humor, and when called for, he knew how to soar poetically or come down suddenly and fiercely on a single crucial word.

Maranzano spoke mainly in Sicilian, but he knew several other languages, including Latin. His Latin he learned while studying to be a priest; Maranzano, like my father, had once attended a seminary school. Perhaps that was why he was such a strict one for manners and decorum. He was as punctilious as an archbishop. . . .

I found him irresistible, he found me refreshing. I was twenty-one years old, and he was about forty. He must have liked having a disciple around him. I liked being around a man of experience. He could talk to me on a high level, as he could with few others among the Castellammarese because they lacked schooling. . . .

In business matters, Maranzano loved perfection. He took great pride in his ledgers, his account books, his records and files. All his books had to be in order, each entry had to be immaculate—an exquisite tapestry of numbers. . . .

I was much like a squire in the service of a knight. Maranzano was my knight. My association with him was like an apprenticeship to see if I had the necessary qualities to be accepted into the society of honored friends—that is to say, a Family.

If Bonanno loved and admired Maranzano, he viewed Masseria differently:

> Though [Masseria] was known as "Joe the Boss," his insa-
> tiable appetite could have won him the nickname "Joe the
> Glutton." He attacked a plate of spaghetti as if he were a
> drooling mastiff. He had the table manners of a Hun.
> Some people eat a lot because they feel happy; others stuff
> themselves because they are nervous. Most people thought
> Masseria ate because he was content, but Maranzano believed
> Masseria was the nervous type of eater, an incomplete man
> inside—the glutton in him compelled him to feed his belly as
> the bully in him was compelled to feed his ego. . . .
>
> I couldn't help comparing my beloved Maranzano with the oaf
> Masseria. Masseria was vulgar, sloppy and puffy. Maranzano
> was refined, taut and intellectual.

Every major gang in New York aligned with either Masseria or Maranzano. Just one independent gang remained: the Luciano outfit, headed by Charlie "Lucky" Luciano (born Salvatore Lucania), the principal bootlegger in New York. Unlike all of the other small-gang leaders, Luciano avoided aligning with either Masseria or Maranzano. He disliked both men, but they had hundreds of soldiers and he had just a few dozen. In time, he would have to choose a side or be killed.

Luciano had no respect for either Masseria or Maranzano. Masseria in his eyes was "short, fat and [had] a round face that was first cousin to a pig." Maranzano: "The old man was nothing better than a big tub of horseshit who was still living with the 'capo' crap he brought over from Sicily, and now he married it to Julius Caesar," Luciano told Gosch, his biographer. Luciano saw himself and his team as smarter and more capable. In 1923, according to Gosch, Maranzano had attempted to win Luciano's loyalty. Luciano was attending the heavyweight-championship fight between

Jack Dempsey and Luis Ángel Firpo at Madison Square Garden. There he was approached by Maranzano, who said, "I have a business proposition for you." "Good. We meet, then?" Luciano replied. "At my club," Maranzano answered.

Two days later, Luciano and Costello, a partner of his, met with Maranzano in Little Italy. They shared pleasantries and red wine. Then Maranzano made Luciano an offer: "As things now stand, we are interfering with each other. We are competing for the same whiskey markets and, unfortunately, killing each other's people. This is foolish and it costs us both too much money and too many good men. This should come to a stop."

"Listen," Luciano said, "you didn't bring me down here to recite the bible of what's right and wrong. What do you got on your mind?"

The reply: "I would like you to join the great Maranzano Family. You would be like my son, like a favorite son. I am prepared to be very generous. You will be like my own bambino."

"You're talking like we're on top of a Sicilian mountain, Maranzano. Let's get down to the ground. What do you want?"

"The young are always in such a hurry. We have considerable legitimate sources of proceeds: we own much real estate in Manhattan.... We are very large importers of foods to satisfy the tastes of our Italian brothers, and our olive oil imports, we anticipate, can be greatly increased with the elimination of an unfriendly Italian competitor in the Bronx."

Maranzano's intelligence was both a gift and a curse: he assumed he had an edge over his competition. But while Luciano lacked Maranzano's formal education and book learning, he had an instinct for people and the wit to outsmart men like Maranzano. He knew that the offer was a setup.

The meeting ended with Maranzano proposing to make Luciano his second-in-command and offering him exclusive rights to the whiskey-distribution business in New York. He had one caveat: Luciano had to drop his Jewish partners, Bugsy Siegel and Meyer Lansky. Maranzano was a traditionalist, preferring to work strictly with Sicilians.

Luciano rejected the offer. Instead, he called a meeting with Masseria, who hated Maranzano even more than he did. Both men knew that Maranzano would not stop until he was the capo di tutti capi. Both men wanted Maranzano dead.

Luciano arrived at the meeting with an ally, a mobster called Joe Adonis. After an underling had patted them down, Masseria wasted no time: "You have a chance to be my friend or the both of you are dead men." Luciano replied, "Joe, you ought to know by now that I'm not afraid of you. I came here to talk business, and Joe A. is here with me as a witness. I'll give it to you straight: okay, I join up with you, but I've got some conditions, Joe. I have to be number two man, above everybody but you. I want a fair piece of the action, and I put into the pot everything that me and my guys do—everything, that is, except not one fucking drop of whiskey." Joe responded, "You dirty, skinny son of a bitch! You're the only paisan in this whole fucking town who ain't afraid of Joe the Boss. Okay, Charlie Lucania, you got a deal."

That deal shifted power in favor of the Masseria Family. Masseria brought in Luciano's entire outfit, including Lansky and Siegel. "Masseria was smart enough to see that even though they was Jews, they could save him a fortune by protecting the robberies the outfit was pulling off all the time in midtown," Luciano wrote later. But "as far as Masseria was concerned, I thought he was a big fat bundle of shit.... If he didn't look like a pig on two legs, I never saw one." Nevertheless, it was official: Luciano was now number-two man in the Masseria Family.

I started to organize his whole fucked-up operation. And except for not getting' the liquor, he didn't have much to complain about. I was giving him my time, Costello threw the slot machines into the deal, [Dutch] Schultz gave me about fifty speaks to toss into the pot as a show of his good faith . . . and he even got Meyer and Bugsy, who was the top protection guys in the country by then.... It was a lot of business to tie up right, but in about six months, I had it all running smooth as silk.

The new arrangement was agonizing for Luciano. Masseria was making more money than he had ever made, but he demanded a larger split and he was constantly on edge. On the surface, he seemed controlling, power hungry, greedy, but actually he was afraid: he knew that Maranzano was working to have him killed. This constant fear made him ever more demanding and distrusting. He even banned his men from carrying guns to get the police off of his back. His disdain for Masseria grew deeper. It was time, Masseria had to be killed, but Luciano knew he had to be careful: Masseria's death would splinter his Family, tilting the balance of power in Maranzano's favor, which would weaken Luciano.

The killing itself, though, would be easy. Masseria was not a forward thinker and could easily be led into his own demise. He controlled through fear, while he himself feared only one person: Salvatore Maranzano. He knew he would not be safe until Maranzano was dead. So, Luciano decided to turn Maranzano's and Masseria's hatred for each other to his advantage. He would send the underworld into chaos while himself seeming neutral.

There was a powerful boss in the Bronx called Tom Reina. He monopolized ice distribution and his gang was the largest and most powerful in Masseria's Family. Reina was loyal, but Masseria began demanding a larger share of his profits and tried to reorganize his gang, knocking him down as boss and putting in his own man, Joseph Pinzolo, as leader instead. Reina would not stand for this.

Luciano had a loyal friend in the mobster Tommy Lucchese, who told him that Reina was secretly plotting to leave Masseria and throw in with Maranzano. This move would weaken Masseria's power and almost certainly guarantee his demise: with Reina in hand, Maranzano would easily claim supremacy in the underworld. Luciano used Lucchese's information to concoct an intricate scheme: if Masseria thought Reina was loyal to him while Maranzano thought Reina was switching sides, and then Reina was killed, his death would spark a war between the two bosses, each one believing that he'd lost one of his own men. As their soldiers killed each other off, they would grow weaker while Luciano— the apparently neutral participant—would grow stronger. In the end, the only men left would be those loyal to Luciano. As Siegel saw the plan, "We got to knock off Reina as soon as possible and Tommy's got to pass the word on to Maranzano that it was a hit from Masseria."

Luciano regretted having to kill Reina, a longtime friend, but he saw no other way to start a war between Maranzano and Masseria. "I picked Vito [Genovese] for the job, with instructions that Reina had to get it face-to-face, according to the rules. I really hated to knock off Tom Reina, and none of my guys really wanted to neither. Reina was a man of his word, he had culture, and he was a very honorable Italian.... But he had to be eliminated so I could keep on living and keep on moving up."

It was February 1930. On Wednesday nights, Reina routinely had dinner in the home of an aunt in the Bronx (Other sources claim he was at the home of Marie Ennis, his mistress). Genovese loaded a shotgun. He waited outside the aunt's home, then fired a cartridge into the face of Tom Reina as he left. Luciano would remember, "Vito told me that when Reina saw him he started to smile and wave his hand. When he done that, Vito blew his head off."

The murder ignited the war Luciano wanted between Masseria and Maranzano, each blaming the other for the hit. This yearlong bloodbath would become known as the Castellammarese War. Now

Luciano began planning to move against Masseria. First, he set up a meeting with Maranzano to discuss a deal. There, he offered to kill Masseria if Maranzano made him his number two and allowed him to take over Masseria's operation. Maranzano agreed.

On April 15, 1931, according to Gosch, Luciano scheduled a lunch with Masseria at a Coney Island restaurant, the Nuova Villa Tammaro. When all the other patrons and the owner were gone, they began to play klob, a Russian card game. After the first hand, Luciano excused himself to use the bathroom. Once he'd left the table, Joe Adonis, Bugsy Siegel, Albert Anastasia, and Vito Genovese came in, guns drawn. Firing 20 rounds, they hit Masseria six times, leaving him slumped over, clutching an ace of diamonds in his right hand.

Accounts of Masseria's death vary. According to Valachi, Vito Genovese, Ciro Terranova, and Luciano were at the restaurant with Masseria, and two shooters, Frank Livorsi and Joseph Stracci, entered and killed Masseria. However, in Nicola Gentile's memoir, *Vita di Capomafia*, Gentile does not place Luciano at the scene.

Luciano's last remaining problem was Maranzano.

With Masseria dead, the hard-fought Castellammarese War was over. Maranzano now sat at the pinnacle of the American Cosa Nostra. "In a few weeks after Masseria stopped being a pig and become a corpse, all Maranzano could think about was the day he was going to be crowned king," Luciano would remember.

Nearly 500 underworld leaders from around the country were summoned to the Bronx for the ceremony that would make Maranzano capo di tutti capi. According to Gosch, the event was held at a banquet hall on the Grand Concourse. Maranzano detailed his plans for the future of Cosa

Nostra and the rules that would hold it all together. "The whole joint was practically covered with crosses, religious pictures, statues of the Virgin and saints I never heard of," Luciano would remember. "Maranzano was the biggest cross nut in the world.... He was an absolute maniac on religion." In attendance were the most powerful made men in the country and the bosses of every Family. This interconnected group made up the underworld's power nationwide.

Joe Bonanno wrote in his book *A Man of Honor*,

> Maranzano, acting as master of ceremonies, welcomed the few hundred people there; only the VIPs had been invited to this exclusive gathering. First off, Maranzano recited the annals of the Castellammarese War. He then apprised us of the reconstitution of leadership in New York, introducing the new Fathers one by one. After a round of applause, Maranzano spoke glowingly about Capone, referring to him at times as Alphonse. Although Capone used to be of the Masseria faction, Maranzano said, he now wanted peace and the enjoyment of a society of friends. In so many words, therefore, Maranzano recognized Capone as the head of the Chicago Family.

According to Joe Valachi,

> The place was packed. There was at least four or five hundred of us jammed in. There were members there I never saw before. I only knew the ones that I was affiliated with during the war. Now there were so many people, so many faces, that I didn't know where they came from. We were all standing. There wasn't any room to sit. Religious pictures had been put up on the walls, and there was a crucifix over the platform at one end of the hall where Mr. Maranzano was sitting. He had done this so that if outsiders wondered what the meeting was about, they would think we belonged to some kind of a holy society. He was just

hanging around, waiting to speak, while the members were still coming in.

He was an educated man. He had studied for the priesthood in the old country, and I understand he spoke seven languages. I didn't know until later that he was a nut about Julius Caesar and even had a room in the house full of nothing but books about him. That's where he got the idea for the new organization.

Under Maranzano's rule, the Five Families of New York would become the primary groups helping him to govern all Cosa Nostra activities in the United States. There were Families in nearly every major city in the country, a far-reaching network that gave the bosses immense power over their members, who had no place to hide. Once you were a member—a made man—the only way out of Cosa Nostra was death. The thousands of members and associates spread nationwide gave the bosses in New York the ability to receive information and win political and judicial favors from powerbrokers all over the country.

"Now it's going to be different," Maranzano told the hundreds in attendance, according to Valachi. "From here on we are going to be divided up into new Families. Each Family will have a boss and an underboss. Beneath them there will be lieutenants, or caporegimes." As far as the soldiers went, Maranzano said, "You will each be assigned to a lieutenant. When you learn who he is, you will meet all the other men in your crew."

"Then he tells us how we are going to operate," said Valachi in *The Valachi Papers*: "If a soldier has the need to see his boss, he has to go first to his lieutenant. If it is important enough, the lieutenant will arrange the appointment. In other words, a soldier ain't allowed to go running all the time to his boss. The idea is to keep everything businesslike and in line."

Maranzano would next go over the rules of Cosa Nostra and the penalty if they were violated:

1. On penalty of death, no member of a Family could break the secrecy of Cosa Nostra, not even within his own home. Cosa Nostra was to be a secret society—a secret government—that as far as the public was concerned did not exist.

2. On penalty of death, members were to obey orders from their direct boss, no matter what the order.

3. On penalty of death, the boss ranked above all else. The boss was God. Members had to come when called. If your wife had an hour to live, you would leave her side if called in by the boss.

4. On penalty of death, members were forbidden to raise a hand to other members. No matter the situation, a member was untouchable unless a boss said otherwise.

5. On penalty of death, members could not intrude on other members' business or covet another member's wife.

6. All grievances were to be forgiven—members had total amnesty from other members.

According to Valachi, there were "other rules where death ain't the penalty. Instead you are 'on the carpet'—meaning you have done wrong and there is a hearing to decide your case."

Having declared himself capo di tutti capi, Maranzano said that each "Family" would be led by a "father" (hence the popular term "godfather") and would follow a hierarchical model:

Capo (boss, father)
Sottocapo (underboss)
Caporegime
Soldier
Associate

The origins of this system are debated. Bonanno and Valachi write of a new organization and structure following the ascension of Maranzano, but their low ranking in Cosa Nostra at the time may have confused their interpretation of his speech: a Cosa Nostra hierarchy system of high and low rank was already in place before 1931. Maranzano was simply reiterating an organizational structure and long-held rules that were understood by higher-ranking members of Cosa Nostra and indeed were already in place in Sicily, where the society originated. The system, though, was not uniformly adopted or enforced, and what Maranzano actually did was mandate that this system become consistent policy among all Cosa Nostra Families in the United States. In this way each Family would have an established administration whose members could interact with other administrations around the country confident in the understanding that they were speaking with trusted, senior-ranked peers.

Maranzano further ordered that each Family boss would report to the boss of bosses—that is, to Maranzano—and would kick up a share of his Family's profits. New York was to be divided into five territories, controlled by five newly created Families: the Bonanno Family, the Gagliano Family, the Luciano Family, the Mangano Family, and the Profaci Family.

Maranzano, though, was notorious for eliminating competition that grew too powerful to control. Luciano knew that his time was limited: when the moment was right, Maranzano would wipe him out. So he hatched a plan to unseat the newly confirmed capo di tutti capi.

For years, Luciano had cultivated relationships with Cosa Nostra's bosses. The powerbrokers of the underworld had long ago pledged allegiance to him; he had trusted relationships with every major Family in the country. Capone, boss of the Chicago outfit, was a longtime friend and supporter. Lucchese, underboss in the Gagliano Family, and Albert Anastasia, underboss in the Mangano Family, were friends as well. Bonanno, Maranzano's staunchest ally—he once said that Maranzano was his hero—had also developed a friendship with Luciano. These relationships made Luciano powerful—even more powerful than Maranzano, the self-anointed boss of bosses.

Many bosses in New York and around the country disliked Maranzano just as Luciano did, but Maranzano was not like Masseria: he was too smart to be led into a restaurant to be killed. Trusting no one, he insulated himself, issuing his orders to only a few of his most trusted men. He spent most of his time surrounded by bodyguards in his Manhattan offices. Getting close enough to him to kill him would be difficult; there would have to be a scheme.

Such schemes were perfect for the mastermind Meyer Lansky.

Lansky asked Luciano for a meeting. He shared that Maranzano had tax problems and that IRS agents visited him regularly at his Park Avenue headquarters. For Lansky, these visits offered a loophole: if a team of killers disguised themselves as federal agents, Maranzano, always looking to appear legitimate, would welcome them into his office. Then they would kill him.

Maranzano was so well insulated that a lot of people didn't even know what he looked like. This created another problem: the shooters would not know who to kill. But Lansky knew that Lucchese was one of the few people Maranzano trusted. He also knew that Lucchese would be glad to see Maranzano dead.

Lansky's plan was to have Lucchese schedule a meeting with Maranzano at around the time the fake agents were to arrive unannounced. As the agents came in, Lucchese would act as the finger man to identify Maranzano. Luciano thought the plan was masterful. It was final—the order was given—Maranzano would be killed.

On September 10, 1931, four men posing as IRS agents arrived at Maranzano's office with a warrant. As Lansky anticipated, the bodyguards there let them in. The hit team immediately pulled their guns, gagging and binding Maranzano's men. They next made their way upstairs to his office, where they found him talking with Lucchese. Maranzano immediately realized what was going on. Lucchese looked at the shooters and nodded: the man in the room was indeed Salvatore Maranzano.

Maranzano fought for his life, battling his assailants bare knuckle, fist to fist. But in the end he lay dead on the floor of his office, stabbed six times, shot four times in the head and chest, and throat slit. The capo di tutti capi was dead. Charlie Luciano was now head of the American Cosa Nostra.

Capone organized a meeting, inviting the bosses from every Family in the country to celebrate the new king. But while the underworld expected the crowning of a new boss of bosses, Luciano had other plans: no one man would rule over Cosa Nostra. Each boss would have autonomy over his own Family, and all disputes and negotiations would be settled by the establishment of a group—the Commission—responsible for the governance of all underworld activity in America. "I explained to them," Luciano told Gosch, "that all the war horseshit was out, that every outfit in every city could be independent but there would be a kind of national organization to hold it all together. I told them we was in a business that had to keep moving without explosions every two minutes; knocking guys off just because they come from a different part of Sicily, that kind of crap, was giving us a bad name and we couldn't operate until it stopped." Thus the Commission was born.

Joe Bonanno would write,

> The Commission was not an integral part of my Tradition.
> No such agency existed in Sicily. The Commission was an
> American adaptation. The Commission would have influence
> but no direct executive power. It had respect only insofar as its
> individual members had respect. More than anything else, the
> Commission was a forum. Modes of power are everywhere
> the same. There were some Fathers I liked and some I detested.
> But I had to try to work with all of them. Also, some of these
> Fathers were more powerful than others, and these men, like
> myself leaders of powerful Families, were entitled to sit on
> the Commission. By participating in these diplomatic con-
> ventions, Families did not give up their independence; they
> were free to do what they wanted. The Commission could
> only exert influence. We agreed to hold national conventions
> once every five years. These conventions served to confirm the
> membership of the Commission for another five-year term.

Just as Luciano rejected the position of boss of bosses, he also refused
the cash-filled envelopes customarily given to a new leader: "I don't
need the money," he said, "I got plenty, and besides, why should
you be paying anything to me when we're all equals?" But the bosses
around the country still saw him as the capo di tutti capi.

The Commission consisted of seven men, all major bosses: the leaders
of the Five Families of New York—Charlie Luciano, Joe Bonanno,
Tommaso Gagliano, Vincent Mangano, and Joseph Profaci—along with
Al Capone of Chicago and Stefano Magaddino of Buffalo. These seven
bosses regulated every Family in the United States. Disputes were settled
through Commission vote. No one boss had more power than another;
power was now shared. Every boss was an equal: one boss, one vote.

The Commission would act as a central governing body over every family in the country:

1. Birmingham, AL: Giuseppe Caternicchia
2. Boston, MA: Gaspare Messina
3. Buffalo, NY: Stefano Magaddino
4. Chicago: Alphonse Capone
5. Cleveland, OH: Frank Milano
6. Dallas, TX: Joseph Piranio
7. Detroit, MI: William Tocco
8. Elizabeth, NJ: Stefano Badami
9. Flint, MI: Tony Cusenza
10. Gary, IN: Paul Palazzolo
11. Kansas City, MO: John Lazia
12. Los Angeles, CA: Joseph Ardizzone
13. Milwaukee, WI: Joseph Vallone
14. New Orleans, LA: Sam Guarino
15. New York City: Joseph Bonanno
16. New York City: Vincenzo Mangano
17. New York City: Salvatore Lucky Luciano
18. New York City: Tommaso Gagliano
19. New York City: Joseph Profaci
20. Newark, NJ: Gaspare D'Amico
21. Philadephia, PA: Salvatore Sabella
22. Pittsburgh, PA: Joseph Siragusa
23. Pittston/Scranton/Wilkes-Barre, PA: Santo Volpe
24. Pueblo, CO: Joseph Roma
25. San Francisco, CA: Francesco Lanza
26. San Jose, CA: Alfonso Conetto
27. Springfield, IL: Vincenzo Troia
28. St. Louis, MO: Thomas Buffa
29. Tampa, FL: Ignacio Antinori
30. Utica, NY: Pietro Lima

The Commission was a success, establishing order and structure within the underworld. Major disputes were now settled through sit-downs. Cowboy-style hits were outlawed; permission had to be sought before a Family member was killed. This helped to prevent bloody wars and allowed Cosa Nostra to grow to unprecedented heights, seizing control nationwide. While there were still high-level assassinations and infighting among members, Cosa Nostra maintained a strong system of order and regulation for the next sixty years, until the fall of America's most infamous don: John Gotti.

THE FIVE EPOCHS
OF THE BOSSES

1 COOKING POT

2 MADE

3 BOSS

4 RED PEPPER

5 ROSE BUSH

The Five Epochs of the Bosses are the five major stages in the life of a Cosa Nostra boss. Epoch 1 is Cooking Pot. Some bosses don't experience it, being born into a higher rank, but for those who do, Cooking Pot is extraordinary training and makes them superior to those who have missed it. Cooking Pot teaches the art of survival. The boss who has experienced it is a "Cooking Pot Boss." The boss who has not is a "Made Boss." A "Made Boss" is a boss who was born into Cosa Nostra privileged with information and protection from a senior-ranking member.

EPOCH 1:
COOKING POT

Exposition

A gangster is a guy who was born without options. He is tough. He is a fighter. He is fearless in the face of danger because danger is all that he has known. He understands that every day could be his last. In the early days of Cosa Nostra, he would have arrived in America as a boy, on a boat, without papers, hiding in a cooking pot. He would have risen from conditions of abject poverty where criminality was rampant. The fathers of Little Italy were day laborers and drunkards but the mothers loved their sons, giving them their all, hoping for a better life for them. Little Italy absorbed the sons, adopted them into *the life*.

Cooking Pot is the genesis. It is when the gangster's *earth was without form, and void; and darkness was upon the face* of the five boroughs. *Cooking Pot* is a slum in Little Italy. It is Mulberry Bend. It is Italian Harlem, 96th to 125th Street. *Cooking Pot* is all things bad. There a man is made a man. His English is broken yet he learns the American way. His hands are roughened, his skin thickened, his backbone straightened. Tough days are every day. The gods of Cosa Nostra lord over the boroughs and their rule is simple: *Be fruitful and multiply, and replenish the earth and subdue it; and have dominion over every living thing that moveth upon the earth.*

Cosa Nostra is a world within a world and its god is the boss. It is governed by its own laws. Formed in Italy, it arrived in America through Ellis Island with no more than a nickel and a dream. The foundation of *the life* was the grit of the early days, the green days.

What gave the gangster his grounding was being the butt of the joke—being laughed at for his trousers, his shoes—and watching mama go without and poppa drink bathtub gin to solace his shame. What gave him his ambitions, driving how he reasoned and what he sought to become, was his green days.

A gangster is born into tough times—born into *Cooking Pot*. His name commands no respect. He fights for survival on the streets. He feeds his kin by work: running numbers for the neighborhood capo, lifting cargo, breaking rules—selling heroin, say, knowing that the boss has said, "If you deal, you die."

To the Family he begins as an unknown. He builds a reputation the way the old-timers did: warring on the mattresses, killing or being killed. He is "stuck, did not have money, getting along on very little," as Joe Valachi said. The old-timers—men like Valachi—earned money with "pinball machines, jukeboxes, horses, and factories." They "never earned a nickel" with the bosses, for a gangster is not born made; a slum child, he fights his way to the making ceremony.

The son of a made guy, on the other hand, is gifted respect. *This thing of ours* ran in his father's blood, his father fought for it, and he can live off his father's work; his name will ring bells in the Five Families, having been celebrated before it was his. But though he may think himself a gangster like his father, he is not a gangster. He is not of *Cooking Pot*. He has inherited the Cosa Nostra that his father risked death for—he is made only by heritage. If he rises to *Boss*, a *Cooking Pot* gangster will easily erase him. A man born made who claims to be a gangster is a liar: he is not a gangster but a racketeer robed in gangster garb. A racketeer is born into respect for his father's name. Respect is granted him for his father's feats. A man born made, born into comfort and respect, will never know the psyche of a gangster.

Cooking Pot is the hardest days you will ever have. A bad day is followed by a day much worse. Hunger is the norm—you sleep on nothing to eat. You don't have a quarter in your pocket. You can't even buy a drink. Look in the cupboard: no coffee, no sugar, no eggs. You have to do "little stickup jobs here and there," as Valachi said. "You stick up subway stations, bank messengers, things like that." You don't like it but you have no choice. And still you make no money. Risking death brings a bigger smile to a gangster's face than the best day of *Cooking Pot*, for if your choices are death or *Cooking Pot*, the choice is easy: better to die and be dead than to be dead while you live.

Cooking Pot is the bad days. Ahead of you is always the possibility of a multiyear sentence: any plan you hatch—a hijacking, say—could bring you ten years without the possibility of parole. There is no life in *Cooking Pot*. You're born dead. Ill-fated. The only way to live is to risk death, hoping to one day be made.

To be a boss, you should first feel the agony of *Cooking Pot*. A boss who has not gone through *Cooking Pot* will lose his grip on his Family. The pain a soldier knows he felt in the green days when times were most brute. It was felt in *Cooking Pot* and no place else. There are no better lessons for *the life* than the lessons of *Cooking Pot*.

In *Cooking Pot* you may be shot or stabbed. You and your crew "take chances," you "go out and steal," you "jeopardize your freedom and your life," according to Valachi. In these times there is no boss, he said, "because there is nothing to be boss about."

A day may come when lawmen surround your car. West and east, north and south, they block the street. You are arrested, charged, convicted, and you serve time, bending to the lawman's rules. These times are your teacher. On your release, you won't repeat the mistakes that got you indicted. These days are *Cooking Pot*. They educate you for all the days to come. Because of *Cooking Pot*, when a soldier graduates to

Made and then to *Boss*, climbing to head a Family, he knows how to lead the regimes and the soldiers therein.

From your time in *Cooking Pot*, you learn that the bullet burns and the blade leaves a scar. You have bullet holes, cuts, bruises, bumps, scabs—but in time you graduate to *Made*. It is what you learned in *Cooking Pot* that makes you a leader. When you rise to *Boss*, you know the soldiers because you were once one of them. You know how they think and what they aspire to. You know that the soldier just wants to earn a buck and buy a place for his children. He doesn't want war, doesn't want murder unending. He wants to live long and then die tending his garden at *Rosebush*, free of prison, fat from vino and pasta.

In *Cooking Pot* nothing is given: in order to have you must take. You see friends kill friends, partners cheat partners—in *Cooking Pot* the end justifies the means. And *Cooking Pot* is where the gangster was born. Yet some learned to be honorable there, to keep their word, and in the streets, a man's word cashes as credit. In *Cooking Pot* the gangster will take a bullet. That is *the life*, and taking bullets is part of the process. It is the path to *Made*.

Everyone bred in *Cooking Pot* will risk his life to get out, and here, relationships are vital. It is relationships that get you sprung from jail. It will be a made guy you know who makes you a "friend of mine," calling you into a room with five other guys to be straightened out—reborn into Cosa Nostra, *this thing of ours*. Once made, you will reminisce about risking your life, and those memories will bring tears to your eyes for you know you started early. By fifteen, you lived by the gun and the knife. You learned.

History

John Joseph Gotti was born in October of 1940 into a poor family in the Bronx. He grew up resenting his father: "Maybe if my father had decided to be a decent human being," he would remember, he and four of his brothers would not all have gone on to become made members of the Gambino Family. Later on, Gotti's debonair and stylish appearance would lead outsiders to call him the "Dapper Don," but Gotti was bred from *Cooking Pot*: "I took myself out of the gutter. I advanced myself. My life was dictated for me. I didn't dictate my life."

Cosa Nostra was Gotti's calling. He began early: when he was fourteen he botched an attempt at stealing a cement mixer, which fell and crushed his toes, leaving him with a limp—a strut that would become a kind of signature, adding to his gangster persona. When he was sixteen he joined a Brooklyn gang, the Fulton-Rockaway Boys. Neil Dellacroce, a powerhouse in the Gambino Family, took him under his wing, mentoring and embracing him as a son. Gotti loved Dellacroce and honored him in life and death. A born leader, Gotti generally followed no one's rules but his own, but with Dellacroce he did as he was told. He was a man of honor.

In 1973, Carlo Gambino sent for Gotti. Gotti was then an associate in the Gambino Family under capo Carmine Fatico. At the meeting, which he attended with his mentor and father figure Dellacroce, Gambino ordered him to organize and carry out a hit on James McBratney, the man responsible for killing Carlo's nephew, Manny Gambino. Gotti's work was subpar: McBratney was killed, but Gotti was identified and arrested. Represented by prominent Cosa Nostra lawyer Roy Cohn, he pleaded guilty to attempted manslaughter and was sentenced to four years in prison. He was released after two.

Gambino, the de facto head of the Commission, ran his Family for two decades, never serving a day in prison. The Gambino Family raked in millions from loansharking, bootlegging, construction, gambling, waste haulage, union racketeering, and extortion. Short in stature at about five foot seven, and gentle in manner, Gambino seemed mild, but he rose to power the way bosses before him did: in 1957, when he was fifty-five, he organized a hit on his boss, Albert Anastasia, who was shot dead while reclining in a barber chair at the Park Sheraton Hotel. Gambino then took control of the Family.

As a teenager, Gambino had worked for "Joe the Boss" Masseria, New York's senior don in the 1920s. Gambino was an earner. He made millions by bootlegging and selling ration stamps on the black market during the Great Depression. He even lounged in gay bars, scouting wealthy homosexuals, then blackmailing them for favors and cash. But he portrayed himself as an everyman. He lived modestly in a blue-collar row house in Brooklyn. He spoke rarely, avoided cameras and media, and did not acknowledge them when they were there. At the age of thirty, he married Catherine Castellano, his first cousin and the sister of Paul Castellano, future boss and nemesis of John Gotti. He was chauffeured about in an old white Buick with a license plate that read "CG1." An immigrant who never graduated high school or became a US citizen, he rose to be the most powerful boss in the country and chairman of the Commission.

In 1976, while watching a Yankees game on TV in a second home on Long Island, Gambino had a heart attack. He died early the next morning, shortly after receiving the last rites from a Catholic priest. Before passing, he appointed Paul Castellano boss of the Gambino Family.

Castellano, known to the underworld as Big Paul, was born in an upper-middle-class neighborhood of Brooklyn on June 26, 1915. He dropped out of school in the eighth grade and began working for his father, Giuseppe, a professional butcher who was also a numbers runner for the Mangano Family. In 1934, Paul was arrested for armed robbery and sentenced to three months in prison. Two accomplices avoided capture; Castellano kept mum on their names. He served his time and was released.

As a cousin and close friend of Gambino's, Castellano was made at an early age and was welcomed into meetings of the bosses. In 1954, in upstate New York, he attended the Apalachin meeting, a summit of the most senior Cosa Nostra leaders in the country. Subpoenaed later to testify before a grand jury about the meeting, Castellano honored omertà and refused. He was cited for contempt of court and sentenced to five years in prison. He served a year and was released.

Yet Castellano's fast track through the ranks of Cosa Nostra made him less gangster, more racketeer.

There are no elections in Cosa Nostra. What leads this thing of ours is blood. To be boss, you must kill the boss above you and all of his loyalists. The Commission will resent you; you will only join it through war. Win the war and the boss's money becomes your money, his rackets become your rackets, his capos become your capos. *Boss* is not given—you kill for it. The prologue to promotion is war. You must put your life on the line, rushing the lobby of the Majestic Apartments on Central Park West, pistol aimed at the head of Frank Costello. If you have not left the father dead on the floor of the Nuova Villa Tammaro restaurant in Coney Island, like Joe Masseria, you are unprepared for *Boss*.

In Cosa Nostra there are earners, shooters, and shooters who earn. An earner is not a boss; a shooter is not a boss. An earner cannot lead shooters because he is not tough enough; a shooter cannot lead earners because he is not smart enough. A future boss is a shooter who earns, a man both tough and smart. He wins the respect of his soldiers because he is tough, but he is also smart. He does not blow his lid. He knows how to earn. He knows when to kill and when not to kill. He is a thinker.

"In our life there's two kinds of guys: there's gangsters, who are thugs, and there's racketeers, who are more like business guys," Castellano once said. "It's very, very rare where you find someone who's both. You're either a thug or a racketeer." The exception, he thought, was Sammy "The Bull" Gravano, who managed both roles and would later remember, "How did I come become both a stone-cold killer and a great business guy that could run unions? It's my upbringing. What I learned from my father, from my mother, from my family—I absorbed that. It never left me how legitimate and how honest they were. How they never lied. That never left me."

He went on, "When I was in businesses, they didn't work, a few of them. I had a fruit and vegetable store, it didn't work. But every time my businesses didn't work, I never thought that I failed in business. I just looked at the businesses and said, 'What did I do wrong that other people could have businesses and succeed? What did I do wrong to not succeed?' So even when I failed, I won. I knew *why* I failed. And it would help me down the road. I knew that. That's what made me both, all, of those things."

Castellano was an earner but an earner is not a boss. A boss is born in the streets—in *Cooking Pot*—as a gangster. He knows both the olive branch and the arrow, is prepared for both peace and war. He respects his soldiers. He knows the reek of urine in an alley: not only has he smelled it, he has left his mark there too. By the time he has risen to *Boss*, every alley in Little Italy has been marked by his bladder.

Reflection

The teachings of *Cooking Pot* are invaluable. Of the five stages of a boss's life, none matters more than *Cooking Pot*.

A boss born into privilege is unlearned. His strength is limited. If two bosses war, the boss bred in *Cooking Pot* will prevail. The *Cooking Pot Boss*, who knows the pain of hunger, will always have an edge over the *Made Boss* born into affluence, his fight fought by his forefathers. For all days past and to come, a *Made Boss* will not overthrow a *Cooking Pot Boss*. A man born into loss has nothing to lose. Winning is his only option.

Cooking Pot is where a boss is molded. There lies desperation, and desperation is a soldier's best teacher.

EPOCH 2:
MADE

Exposition

Made is the good times. In *Made* you have "a whole enterprise behind you—a whole army," said Joe Valachi. "It's like having a license" to do anything. *Made* justifies the tough times of *Cooking Pot*, the days of going without. "You are only made once. If you live a hundred years, it will be just that once," said Valachi.

Tough times are a certainty of *the life*, but in *Made*, every day is a day you have prayed for. Your name is respected. Your car is imported. Your cash is plentiful. *Made* is a plush home in New Jersey, away from the city where you and the Five Families toil. *Made* is when the boss knows your name: "Hey, Joe Cago, don't look so sad," Lucky Luciano told Joe Valachi, calling him by his nickname. *Made* is when anyone who wants to make a move on you needs permission. There are rules: any man lays a finger on you, the penalty is death. *Made* is the high life. "You can lie, you can cheat, you can steal, you can finagle, you can cause a ruckus. You can kill people legitimately. You can do any goddamn thing you want and nobody can say anything about it," according to Bonanno Family member Lefty Ruggiero.

In *Made*, you can cheat with your *gumada* and no one will tell your wife. You can have four children—two with your wife, two with your *gumada*. You will have it all: "manhood and respect from the Family," said Ruggiero. "Respect for your friends, respect for your children, and respect for your wife when she walks the street."

Once you have made it to *Made*, life is never the same. Winning lasts a long long time—a time so long that you may forget *Cooking Pot*. But a man should not distance himself from those memories. No matter how happy the time, every day a made guy lives a bullet away from losing everything he has won, for in Cosa Nostra there is always a man beneath you who wants what you have gained and there is always a man above you wondering if you are growing too powerful—wondering whether or not he should kill you. Indictments and juries also stand by, awaiting a made guy's downfall. *Made* is good times, but *Made* misleads: it makes a man believe that what is will always be.

In *Made*, you have a voice in the boss's ear. You are respected in all Five Families. If you are upped from soldier to caporegime, you are called to the sit-downs and you lead a crew of up-and-comers who hope one day to mimic your feats. You can tell a reporter, as Gambino Family boss Jackie "Nose" D'Amico did, "I'm insignificant. I'm not important. I take the 4 train, the 5 train, the 6 train. That's the only way I travel. I don't have a chauffeur-driven car." It matters not—what matters is that you are made.

There are two types of made man: the humble and the arrogant. You can be meek and mild or boastful and boisterous. The arrogant die when problems come, while the humble face their troubles and beat them. They live long and fruitful to the end, where the maker of the heavens decides their fate. The humble keep everything, the arrogant lose everything. When you are made, leave your ego at the door of the making ceremony—yet what graduates a man from *Cooking Pot* to *Made*, and from *Made* to *Boss*, is ego. What makes a man breaks a man: ego also marches you from *Boss* to *Red Pepper*, a place of trial. The arrogant make short-term gains only to lose everything in *Red Pepper*, where defeat humbles them. And by the time they are humbled, it is too late: they have already lost their family and the Family, their lives and *the life*.

The arrogant are loud and overbearing. They have an inflated sense of self-worth. They have five lire yet say they have ten. They call two years in prison "ping-pong time." To have ego is to like yourself more than the brotherhood and to see others as objects, not people. If a man is arrogant in *Made*, he will be arrogant in *Boss* and *Red Pepper*. The humble have ears to heed, eyes to witness, cognition to reason; the arrogant hear and see nothing but themselves and think just one way, *their* way. They are egotists today, tomorrow, and all days to follow. They have egos bigger than all Five Families.

Made develops ego. *Made* brings shoeboxes stuffed with money and a stature that makes a man's name ring like a bell. A made man who is not humble thinks himself invulnerable. He believes he cannot be beat. But invincible no man can be.

Be wise. Don't be the fool that *Made* can make you.

Since its inception, Cosa Nostra has been self-interested and cruel. *The life* is precarious. The capo of today is on the shelf tomorrow, an outcast from all Five Families. Better not to have been made at all than to be put on the shelf. Better to die by the bullet; that way you feel no pain, you are instantly done. But to die on the shelf is torture. It is to die a slow death. You die on the shelf when the bosses hate you.

On the shelf, you lose everything you ever knew. You are ejected from the world to which you swore an oath. You have no standing or value and no social place. The money you have is all you will ever have. You are persona non grata. No made guy will speak to you. When on the shelf, you are in an unknown world—something new to your psyche. You don't leave home because you have nowhere to go. Your barber was an associate of the Family; your favorite restaurant is where all the made guys go. You are shunned at that restaurant and shunned by your barber. And even though you're on the shelf, the boss still owns you. He decides what is permitted and forbidden to you. On the shelf, your options are sparse: go sit in your house. Go nowhere you would be seen. Sit in your house and rot until you die. If the boss loved you at all, he would have gifted you the honor of a bullet in the head. To die by the bullet is not so shameful in Cosa Nostra.

Before a man reaches *Made*, his life should be in order. *Cooking Pot* produces orderly, disciplined men, but the allure of *Made* is so strong that it can disorder and inflate even the orderly and humble. In *Made*, a man who once knew his way can get lost in his gains. He can stagger through his successes.

In *Made*, you will learn to keep a large stash of dollars because payola is the way you get things done. It is how you pay the commissioner to keep the police off your back. *Made* teaches you that every man has a price. You yourself may be tempted to break the rules—by selling heroin, say—but your boss can never know, for if you get caught, you will be killed. The rule of the Family is "You deal, you die," but you might break the rule because dealing in heroin turns a big profit. Those profits will make the boss see you as an earner. You dress dapper, because it is easier to earn a dollar in a suit. Also, a suit will make the soldiers want to be like you.

Made "is the highest honor [Cosa Nostra] can give you," says Henry Hill (Ray Liotta) in Martin Scorsese's 1990 film *Goodfellas*. "It means you belong to a Family." It means you are loved by everyone. Even the cops love you: "They didn't care whether I was a crook, a criminal, whatever," said Sammy Gravano. "They got four envelopes from me every week: one for the division, one for the precinct cops, another for the precinct detectives, and one for the sergeants." In *Made*, when you get pinched— caught with a gun—you can do what Gravano did: "I walked right into the precinct and I pulled the arrest card out of the typewriter and ripped it up. I said to the detectives, 'Listen, no pinch. I'll give you $2,500 and I want the gun back.'" In *Made*, nothing sticks. "What counted, what was real, was the money." So you're caught illegally carrying a gun? For $2,500 the charges are voided and you can tell the cop, "I want my gun back." The cop will hand it back "at the luncheonette, the usual spot where we used to meet."

To be made, you must swear an oath. You are choosing a new path, *the life*. Here, "Your life is not your own. You are property of somebody. You are property of this Cosa Nostra entity—this Cosa Nostra that goes back hundreds of years. You are property of theirs," according to Gambino caporegime Michael "Mikey Scars" DiLeonardo. Cosa Nostra is not a business; it is not a club. "It is a subculture from everything else that exists. It is a secret society. There is one way in and one way out—on a slab." Violate the rules of this thing and Cosa Nostra "is one long memory." It will not forget that you broke a rule. "Cosa Nostra does not forget," said DiLeonardo. You will be killed. And if you are not killed in this lifetime, you will suffer in the life after, where your soul will burn in hell like the saint.

Made teaches you to put in your all. Investing totally is what will get you to *Made*, and once there, the same investment will get you to *Boss*. You will kneel to your boss and kiss his ring without hesitation. You will watch your *goombata*, your mentor and friend, someone you love and trust, godfather to your children. From him you learn: to rise you must first submit.

The soldier advances by being a good runner for the capo. In *Made* you do the same. You learn never to speak in the dark of the boss's ear. You give it to him straight, for *Made* will teach you that when you shoot a boss, you shoot him in the face—out of respect. You make it to *Made* by aligning with the highest ranked. Since the police commissioner has higher rank than the cop, you bribe the commissioner—now you have a handle on all the cops.

Once you're in *Made, the life* pays handsomely, giving you everything you've dreamed of. Once in *Made*, to drive your Mercedes you first have to move your Cadillac and your Lincoln parked in front of it. For the privacy to make love to your *gumada* you have to get the nanny and the maid out of the house. Such difficult problems! Forget about it.

The phone does not stop ringing: bankers are calling, asking what you want to do with your cash. You are close to the top, to *Boss*, where you answer to none. *Boss* is where you set the rules. But you will learn: the only path to *Boss* is to kill whoever lives there and take his Family as your own.

History

After Gotti's release from prison for the McBratney killing, in 1977, he was made and promoted to caporegime. A loyalist and friend of Dellacroce's, Gotti began running his own crew, based in the Bergin Hunt & Fish Club in Ozone Park, primarily operating street rackets under the blue-collar helmet of the Family.

An admirer of Albert Anastasia, Gotti was as pure a gangster as Vito Genovese, the most vicious and ruthless of all gangsters of all times. For Don Vitone, nothing came before Cosa Nostra, and the same was true of the Dapper Don: "I chose my side over forty years ago, when I was sixteen years old. I'm going to go out of this world with a smile on my face, because I believe what I believe."

From *Cooking Pot* to *Rosebush*, Gotti was purest Cosa Nostra. More than he was a father, husband, brother, or friend, he was a gangster. "He would shoot you in a fucking hot minute," said Gravano. His oath to Cosa Nostra was more sacred to him than God and family. The Family had higher authority.

"My father lived that life 24/7," said Gotti's son Junior. "In fact, his wife and kids were second to the streets. He loved it; he loved the code. He loved the action. He loved the chase. My father had to be out there— out there in the city. No other city can do for John but New York City. Because it never slept. There was always action."

As a made guy supported by Dellacroce, an old-timer respected by both the Young Turks and the Mustache Petes (the newer and older genera-tions of mobsters), Gotti was one of the most respected caporegimes in the Gambino Family. He had successfully carried out a hit on behalf of Gambino, the most powerful boss in all the Five Families and head of the Commission. This gave Gotti great status in the New York underworld.

According to Colombo Family capo Michael Franzese, "You could never let John Gotti think that you won an argument. His ego wouldn't allow it. So you had to figure out a way to outsmart him—to make him think he won but you actually got what you wanted. I knew that he could never believe that I was winning."

Once made, and now the Family's senior capo, Gotti lived by the rules not of *the life* but of John Gotti. He did what he wanted. His boss, Castellano, had banned the sale of narcotics; according to DiLeonardo, Castellano had gone so far as to set up "a committee to go around pulling in all the skippers two at a time with their crews and telling them the edict against dealing drugs, that if you are caught, you will be killed." But Angelo Ruggiero, a long-time Gotti loyalist and member of Gotti's crew, was selling heroin by the kilogram.

"Anytime you are sent for by the boss of your family," Castellano once told Gravano, "you must come in. If your child is dying and has only twenty minutes to live, and your boss sends for you, you must leave that kid and come. If you refuse, you will be killed. . . . I'm the boss. I'm the father of the family. I am your God." (All this Gravano revealed in his autobiography, *Underboss*, of 1997.) Cosa Nostra is a brotherhood, an honored society of men who respect each other. In that brotherhood "you got to be proud of who you are and fight for it," Gotti believed. To you it is the highest government in the world, and the boss is God. The Holy Trinity ranks below the boss. The boss is the King of Kings, the God of Gods. No made guy speaks ill of the boss. Better to cut out your tongue than to speak ill of the boss. For speaking against the boss, the penalty is death.

Gotti had sworn a blood oath to abide by the rules, but he did not hide his contempt for Castellano. He aired his grievances loudly. It was no secret: Gotti wanted the boss dead. Only then could he ascend to the apex of the Gambino Family.

Ruggiero shared Gotti's disdain for Castellano: "Paul don't know what it's like to be on the street without a quarter in your pocket." Ruggiero was picked up on FBI wiretaps calling Castellano a "pansy" and a "milk drinker," and accusing his boss of lounging in his $3 million mansion, masturbating with the Family underboss, Tommy Bilotti.

Dellacroce was a Cosa Nostra originalist. He had been groomed in *the life* under the original doctrine of "The boss is the boss"—the boss is God. Dellacroce had earned his place in the society by dirtying his hands, honoring the code of omertà, and working the street rackets. For him, the rules of *the life* preceded everything else. They were not to be defied. On his deathbed, in an intense exchange with Gotti and Ruggiero, Dellacroce schooled them for their defiance of Castellano: "You see, that's why I says to you before, 'You don't understand Cosa Nostra.' Cosa Nostra means that the boss is your boss."

Castellano represented the curve in Cosa Nostra, the period when leadership began to move from Italian immigrants to first-generation Italians born in America. The early dons—Albert Anastasia, Joe Bonanno, Frank Costello, Tommaso Gagliano, Carlo Gambino, Vito Genovese, Tommy Lucchese, Charlie Luciano, Joe Magliocco, Vincent Mangano, Salvatore Maranzano, Joe Masseria, Manfredi Mineo, Giuseppe Morello, Joe Profaci, Tom Reina, Frank Scalise— were Italians from the motherland. The shift in Cosa Nostra, the rise of the first-generation Italians, marked a change in the tradition. Cosa Nostra was now being led by Americanized dons.

Castellano had been schooled by the old-timers but he was not respected the way they were. As a businessman he understood construction and labor unions and he worked well with the business-minded racketeers of the Family. But the hard-knock gangsters who still largely made up the Family did not see themselves in Paul. A lot of them thought he was greedy. The Dellacroce faction in particular loathed Castellano, considering him self-serving and indifferent to the overall Family interest. "He wasn't a gangster and he didn't understand gangsters. He didn't understand what the fuck it was to be broke, to have to go out and rob. He didn't understand what a gangster was all about. He didn't understand gangsters like John Gotti and Angie Ruggiero, or me or Frank DeCicco," said Gravano.

Castellano was covetous. He was once overpaid $40,000 owed to Gravano: "Paul," Sammy said, "I believe Louie Giardino gave you forty last week. That was mine. You were paid and the union was paid." "Shhh! Don't bring it up to me anymore. I'll bring it up to you," Castellano replied. After the meeting, the powerhouse capo Frank DeCicco told Gravano, "Gee, Sammy, you're so fucking dumb. This guy gets his hands on money, he never gives it back. He's never bringing up that forty again."

Gotti heatedly opposed Castellano and thought the Family would be better off without him. After Ruggiero was indicted on federal narcotics charges, in 1983, Gotti further believed that Castellano was going to break up Gotti's crew and reduce his rank from capo to soldier. Gotti was largely protected by his friend and mentor Dellacroce, who was the underboss of the Castellano Family, but that protection ended when Dellacroce died, in 1985. At that point Gotti quickly began plotting to kill Castellano. Sounding out trusted members of the Five Families, he found support in four of the five. He did not seek approval from the Genovese Family, arguably the most powerful, because Castellano was close with Vincent "Chin" Gigante, boss of the Genoveses. Gotti concluded, "Fuck Chin. If it comes down to it, we'll go to war with them."

It was final: Castellano had to go, and Tommy Bilotti too. Gotti gave the order. It was time for a killing.

Reflection

As *Made* makes, so *Made* breaks. Of the many men made, few rise to *Boss*. Once made, a rational man will cool his ambition and be satisfied with the rank he has won. If made, why aspire to more? Stay put. Only the foolish want the rank of boss.

In *Made*, a man can be upright. He can live the good life. He can be a father to his children, a good poppa. He can be a principled husband—loyal, devoted to his wife. His mistress—he is devoted to her too. She smiles ear to ear, for he foots her bills and sleeps in her bed three times a week. The mistress and the wife share a good made guy.

A made guy knows his limits. A boss does not. If ten made men try to be boss, one will occasionally succeed but most often ten will perish, and perish brutally. Maybe they have their testicles chopped off; maybe they're shot dead in front of their children. *Made* "is a wonderful life, but it's very unpredictable. There are many ways to screw it up," said Castellano. In *Made*, don't go for *Boss*. Much will come to you in *Made*, but once in *Boss*, where do you go? So accept *Made* as your life. Relish it. Be content and don't look for more, for *Boss* is a world beyond the world, where the lights are nowhere so bright, but also nowhere so dull.

A made guy who tries to be boss screws up his life. Choose wisely.

EPOCH 3:
BOSS

Exposition

Boss is a world beyond anything you ever dreamed. It is the uppermost point of all things *our thing*. Go to the mountain. Stand at its peak. Once there, marvel, for you are at *Boss*—the senior rank of all human existence. All that you see, and more that you don't—the faraway and the unseen—are under the governance of *Boss*. Nowhere is higher. Once there, no more can be gained in *the life*—from *Boss* a man only goes down. For the rest of the boss's life, the brotherhood will be a cul-de-sac.

While *Made* times are good times, a million days of *Made* do not compare to one day of *Boss*. If the option is there, far better to live one day of *Boss* than 100 years of *Made*, for a made guy lives only for today, the now, whereas a boss lives for all days to come, until the sun burns out and Earth is no more. A boss lives forever.

So few men rise to *Boss* that to think you can is a castle in the air. So when a made guy reaches that rank, he has defied all logic and reason.

All men submit to *Boss*. *Boss* is when you make the rules, enforce the rules, break the rules—do what you want with the rules. The rules are the boss's jurisdiction. If he breaks them, so be it: the boss is the boss. He is the decider, both judge and jury. All men obey the boss's order. What is is what the boss decrees. Bad is good: the boss is justice even when wrong.

As *Boss*, you do what you want. Dare a man challenge you, be he that foolish, consequences will follow. The boss is God, deciding whether he lives or dies. Men line up begging for a favor; the boss pulls a string here, a string there. If he slaps a man's face, the man will apologize and turn the other cheek.

The soldiers respect the boss. They do anything he tells them. In his presence, they may even stutter. That is how they think about the boss: they are weakened by the mere sight of him.

In *Boss* you have caporegimes, a couple of dozen. You have soldiers in the hundreds. If they weep or grumble, you are deaf, for you have been through it all twice multiplied. All pain that humans feel, the boss felt to become the boss.

The boss's face is disfigured: nerve damage. Over 100 stitches to fix a wound from a beating and stabbing. They call him "Lucky" now. He has been through two Cosa Nostra wars; he won them both. No man, no soldier, no capo or underboss has the right to howl at the boss.

When the boss arrives, he arrives chauffeured. His ring is kissed. He is gifted envelopes of cash. The underboss opens the Mercedes door for him and holds an umbrella when it rains. He always walks one step behind the boss, never ahead. Everyone walks at the boss's pace; the boss does not walk at theirs.

While *Boss* is a wonderland, it is also a time in the crosshairs. *Boss* is a position of one. Thousands wish for *Boss*, but not one can get it as long as the boss is there. Accordingly, he is loathed.

A soldier has a nickel and a woman. When the boss walks in, the soldier's failure is on display: as his woman looks on, he must kneel, kiss the boss's ring, and give the boss his nickel. And if the boss likes the soldier's woman, he will leave with her too.

Don't confuse *Made* and *Boss*. *Made* is a good life; a made man is respected and wields power. But made men submit to *Boss*. The boss sets the rules that oblige the made man. Many made guys don't know the boss, it is not unusual: a soldier may be in Cosa Nostra ten years and never see the boss.

A capo thinks himself a boss. He has twenty soldiers to give orders to, twenty soldiers giving him envelopes, twenty soldiers asking his permission for everything they do. Even the soldiers think the capo is a boss. But no matter what the capo says or does, for the boss he is no more than a buffer. He gives the boss his devotion, takes the soldiers' hard-earned end and gives it to the boss. Then, a fool and a fall guy, he serves 100 years in the penal as the boss's dupe.

The capo is a fake boss. He thinks himself shrewd, but if he had an IQ point in his noodle, he would have killed the boss at the making ceremony. Why does the capo kiss the boss's ring when the boss is fat and eats pasta in his Staten Island mansion while the capo and his soldiers have not a penny? Dumb dupe. Why not shoot the boss dead, then unionize the regime? Aren't the soldiers the ones who bring in the Family's money? The boss gets *niente* unless the capo turns it in. The capo's noodle is empty. He thinks himself a boss until the actual boss walks in.

The capo "has a 100 percent edge over the soldier. The soldier has to do it himself," said Joe Valachi. The soldier has to bring in money while the capo takes money from him. "The way the machine works is captains in the hierarchy eat through the associates and soldiers," said Michael DiLeonardo. They have to support the capos, who in turn support the bosses.

Upping a soldier to capo is the key to a boss's power. Receiving new powers from the boss, the capo gives the boss his allegiance and enforces the rules.

Don't be fooled by the bravado of the capo. The capo is not a boss. He is a shrewd buffoon, crazier than his soldiers. A boss must be a genius, for only a genius could convince a made guy to put his life and freedom at risk by going on a heist only to turn over his profit to the boss.

The boss is a mastermind. He is an architect of men. Though he is just one man, he inspires made guys by the hundreds to kill on his behalf, to turn over their earnings, to come when called even knowing they may die. The boss shakes his soldiers down for everything they have. He is an engineer of the ignorant, informed among a mass of uninformed, a master among slaves. He orders his underboss how to rule his soldiers: "Keep them broke. Keep them hungry. Don't make them too fat," Gotti told Gravano.

Boss is grand but boss means boss. Troubles come to the boss in unmanageable numbers. The boss has no friends, for he is envied by all. Their praise is deceit. Worry and weariness are the norm. *Boss* is both bliss and shit, and a whole lot of the latter. But if *Boss* is ever for the taking, take it, no matter what comes with it, for it is better to be a boss than to be owned by one. No matter the troubles of *Boss*, no life is more alive than a boss's. It is a life few men know.

A boss will suffer and die more brutally than a made man, but that will not deter him from his duty as godfather. He will own his role. He will settle on his fate. The boss knows that his calling is to die facing the gun, eyes wide open. At the making ceremony, he swore by blood oath to live with the gun and to die by the bullet. What frightens a boss is not death but dying without honor. When he and the revolver eventually make merry, he only hopes to get it straight in the face, according to the rules.

For a boss to last, he must mix with the soldiers—must stay close to any troubles brewing in the Family. But knowing no place or person is safe for speech, he must say nothing of substance. To keep the Family in line, harsh rules are required; a boss will have to kill a couple of men to keep his couple of hundred men in order. But the boss's hands must be clean. Dirty work is for the underboss.

To last, the boss must pay his soldiers well, and when he speaks, he must speak in a tongue familiar to them. If soldiers are not to be confused, the boss must speak in a way they understand. *Boss* talk is reserved for the bosses.

A boss should live modestly. He should make all the talented men in Little Italy, using their skills to heighten the Family's powers. Above all, a boss should never turn up his nose at the public. The public is to be respected—loved. When a boss reaches *Red Pepper* he will need his public to sway the jury and fight the prosecution and the press.

History

After John Gotti had Paul Castellano killed, he restructured and reunited a Family that had been opposed to its former boss. Gotti "put the gangsters back in charge," according to Gotti underboss Sammy "The Bull" Gravano. The soldiers and caporegimes had a home again: in their new boss they saw someone who knew what it meant to be a gangster.

With the flamboyance of Capone and the cunning of Anastasia, Gotti rose from Howard Beach to the cover of *Time* magazine. "Mafia on Trial," the headline read. *Boss* promoted Gotti to fame. Chauffeured in a black Mercedes, dressed in hand-tailored suits, signing autographs, he was a celebrity gangster, sought after not only by the most powerful government in the world but by its press and people.

Once an old wives' tale, a witch hunt by the American judiciary, with Gotti Cosa Nostra emerged from the shadows. If even the slightest hint of doubt remained as to its existence, with Gotti that doubt died. A secret society became a public conspiracy. A private entity became a known organization. The "Mafia" became a household name.

According to Sammy the Bull, Gotti "used to get up around eleven or twelve o'clock in the afternoon. He had somebody picking out his clothes. He used to have a barber come every single day to give him a haircut and to cut the hairs in his nose. It was a play to him. It was a performance for the media. He went in a restaurant one time and he liked the wine that was $50 per bottle. And he made Joe Watts go grab the owner and raise it on the menu to $200 per bottle because people knew that John Gotti liked that wine. He was obsessed with the whole image of himself."

Gravano later turned state's evidence and went to prison. In a television interview after he got out, he described a meeting he had had at a restaurant with Gotti and Gambino associate Joe "The German" Watts. A nearby couple stared at Gotti to such an extent that Sammy was unnerved and asked Gotti whether their bodyguard should approach the couple's table. Gotti replied, "No, no, Sammy. That's my public."

Gotti's public would later revolt against the judiciary and the media, taking his side. When he was finally convicted at trial, a supporter protested, "This government is no good. He should be out. He's a good guy; he does a lot for the community. They put him away for nothing." Gotti's daughter Victoria told the press, "My father is the last of the Mohicans. They don't make men like him anymore—they never will."

While Gotti was brutal—a gangster—Gravano was an earner. In fact he was the chief earner in the Gambino Family, turning in anywhere from $1.2 million to $2 million a year. He earned by controlling unions and construction. He was also the Family's chief enforcer,

organizing eight murders on order or approval from Gotti, including the murder of Paul Castellano.

Gotti's allegiance to Cosa Nostra was clear on the night of December
24, 1988, when he inducted his son John Junior into the Family.
When Junior was made, Gotti was "as proud as a father would be
if his son just made All-American," according to Junior. Not even
the boss's son, though, could escape Gotti's belief in the rules and in
the consequences of their violation. Shortly after Junior was made,
Gotti ordered that his lifelong friend Angelo Ruggiero was to be put
on the shelf. No Family member was to engage with him. But Junior
violated dictate. Gotti was livid: "Your Uncle Angelo—I declared
him persona non grata. I put him on the shelf. Me, I issued a rule.
Nobody is allowed to see him. Nobody! Who the fuck are you to
violate my fucking rule? I fucking told you something. I told everybody something! My rules are the gospel—that's the way it is. Who
are you to violate that? Don't ever let it happen again. Don't let me
hear it happens again. Pray that I don't know about it."

Gotti became the most recognized gangster since Al Capone. Neither
death nor a life sentence was a deterrent. "I don't give two fucks about
myself going to jail. This is going to be a Cosa Nostra until I die. Be it
an hour from now or be it tonight or a hundred years from now when
I'm in jail, it's going to be a Cosa Nostra."

In a *60 Minutes* interview, Junior recalled conversations with his
father about the inevitable fate of Cosa Nostra members: "He hated
money. If a guy was saving money or putting money away, he would
say, 'What's on his mind? What's he got planned? At the end of the
day we're all going to jail. What's he going to do with that money?'
He felt that anybody who really truly lived in the streets, at the end
of the day, you got to die or go to jail." Recognizing this inevitable
fate, Gotti prepared his Family for it: "Tomorrow I want to call all
our skippers in. I'm going to tell them: 'I'm the *rappresentante* until

I say different. Soon as anything happens to me, I'm off the streets, Sammy is the acting boss.' I'm going to make our skippers understand that. This is my wishes, that if I'm in the fucking can, this Family is going to be run by Sammy. I'm still the boss. If I get fifty years, I know what I got to do. But when I'm in the can, Sammy's in charge."

Like Carlo Gambino, Gotti lived modestly, in a simple row house in Howard Beach. He resented Castellano for living in a big Staten Island mansion far from the soldiers. "All I want is a good sandwich. You see this sandwich here—this tuna sandwich? That's all I want—a good sandwich."

Gravano, on the other hand, who by his own account "made millions in construction and shylocking, . . . had a house on Staten Island worth about a half a million." He "had a thirty-acre horse farm in New Jersey." He "owned the office building" that housed his construction company.

Gotti stayed close to where the soldiers worked their rackets. Monies earned were shared among the soldiers with the capos keeping the larger share. Money came in and went out: when Joseph Gallo and Joseph "Joe Piney" Armone were convicted on racketeering charges, in 1987, Gotti paid $135,000 for their appeal. He spent $17,500 on printing minutes and preparing briefs; shortly after, he got hit with another $12,800. Legal fees were immense. The lawyers, not the Family, wound up with the money. Gravano once told Gotti that his lawyers, Gerald Shargel and Bruce Cutler, "were overpriced, overpaid, and they underperformed." Gotti himself said that the Gambino Crime Family should be renamed the "Shargel, Cutler, and Whattaya-call-it Crime Family."

Gotti won three consecutive acquittals on government indictments. He became a nationally recognized celebrity. Because the government was unable to make a case stick, the media rechristened the Dapper

Don the Teflon Don. A darling of the public, Gotti was a ratings and sales booster for TV and newspapers. But his *Time* cover and front-page news stories did not warm the hearts of the bosses on the Commission. Vincent "Chin" Gigante, boss of the Genovese Family, resented Gotti for his public persona and for killing Castellano without Commission approval.

Historically, Cosa Nostra leaders avoided notoriety, but Gotti embraced it. His celebrity weakened his Family and the underworld as a whole.

Gotti now held court at the Ravenite Social Club on Mulberry Street in Little Italy. Every capo in the Family was required to report there every week. This unusual practice eased the job of law enforcement: "What John did is basically unprecedented in organized crime. Prior to his reign of the Gambino Family, everybody was much more secretive. This was his style; this was his flair; this is what brought him down," said FBI supervisor George Gabriel. "No boss ever made the whole Family show up at any one place, in plain view, in plain daylight. The mob doesn't work that way. They don't show up all at once and make life easy for us."

The government put listening devices all through the Ravenite. But no matter what pressures were mounting, Gotti continued to hold court in full view. Gambino capos, the Gambino underboss, and the Gambino consigliere continued to filter in and out of the infamous social club, and to pace up and down Mulberry Street discussing Family matters. To Gotti's surprise, the FBI was listening in on every word.

Reflection

Boss is not the glitz that it seems. High times pass in a blink. Among all fables, *Boss* is the greatest of all. *Boss* makes a man lose his footing and imagine himself above *the life*. But as far back as the Black Hand, *the life* is *the life*. No one is immune, whether boss or soldier. The bullet that pierces the soldier can pierce the boss. The law can arrest the high as well as the low. So during high times, stay grounded. On the ground, it is easier to distinguish the real from the forged.

A target has one bull's-eye. Just one. So it is with Cosa Nostra: one Family, one boss, one bull's-eye. Every bullet is aimed at that bull's-eye. You can dodge a bullet for twenty years, but in time the bullet and the bull's-eye will come together. So, as boss, make every day count, for once you get to *Boss* there is no way back.

EPOCH 4:
RED PEPPER

Exposition

Red Pepper is when the boss faces his greatest test. It is when his kingship is challenged. It is when everything he has worked his whole life for is at risk. Every boss, whether weak or strong, has a period of *Red Pepper*: the soldiers are in revolt, the capos are going to jail or, worse, cooperating with the law, and indictments are coming down on the most important members of the Family.

Whatever a boss's brilliance and forward thinking, a day will come that will tax him. The power and respect begot in *Boss* will not lessen his angst. His cash coffer, no matter how big, will not conquer his troubles. *Red Pepper* divorces the capo from the capo di tutti capi, the strong from the supremely strong. It is character, inner strength, and relinquishment of ego that guide a boss through *Red Pepper*. A bull-headed, egocentric boss will not prevail. He will be sentenced to life in a supermax prison or stripped of his Family by a bullet from an ambitious caporegime.

The rules that graduate a boss from *Cooking Pot* to *Made*, and from *Made* to *Boss*, have no bearing in *Red Pepper*. To survive, a boss will have to find a new strategy clean of everything that made him boss. The rules of *Made* don't apply in *Red Pepper*. Put ten bosses in *Red Pepper* and nine will revert to the rules that made them boss; that will be futile. In 1,000 *Red Peppers*, no boss will escape by using the rules that got him to *Boss*.

In *Red Pepper*, a boss will begin to wonder whether his gains—fortune, fame, respectability, influence—were worth the pain that followed them. *Red Pepper* is the worst time of a boss's life. It hurts more than *Cooking Pot*.

Don't confuse *Cooking Pot* with *Red Pepper*. *Cooking Pot* is poverty and disorder, a tough life. But *Red Pepper* is rotting in a six-by-eight-foot barred cell, drinking from the toilet—same water you move your bowels in. It is your name on a federal indictment: *United States of America v. Boss*. You fight the case knowing that the chance of winning it is as likely as Salvatore Maranzano rising from the grave, drinking vino, and dancing a tarantella with Joe Masseria. *Red Pepper* is "going over the car every day, from the front bumper to the rear bumper, real careful," as Lucky Luciano said, because the Cosa Nostra that you built and loved—dedicated your life to—might plant a bomb in it. It is staring down the barrel of a pistol when a hitman bellows "This is for you" before he puts a bullet in your cranium.

Red Pepper is a period of unmatched agony: civil war in the Family, legal troubles mounting, tossing and turning at night wondering whether or not you should kill your underboss because he is growing too strong. *Red Pepper* threatens the boss's ability to control his Family. No preparation readies a boss for it. These days are fought real time—live action. You dodge the bullets as they come. And in the end, a boss prevails or dies. He either holds on to his Family with an even stronger grip or is no longer boss.

In Cosa Nostra, most who rise to *Boss* will ultimately fall. *Cooking Pot* and its teachings will help them land. A life begun at *Made*, on the other hand. will make *Red Pepper* harder, for all of us are grounded in our beginnings and a man born into *Made* knows only good times. He does not know struggle or the smell of a Bensonhurst alleyway. If he put in time in *Cooking Pot*, though, he is ready for the trials of *Red Pepper*. When tough times come, he is more likely to prevail.

No matter how grand *Boss* life is and no matter how well prepared a boss is, *Red Pepper* will come. Whether the boss is beloved or spurned is irrelevant: you can be Don Carlo Gambino—all Five Families loved Don Carlo—you can be Frank Costello, be Tommy Lucchese—it matters zip. The anguish of *Red Pepper* is a certainty of *Boss*.

Everyone in Cosa Nostra knows what it is to have a problem. Associates have problems, soldiers too. All the caporegimes know what it is to have a problem. But only a boss knows *Boss* problems. Since few men make it to *Boss*, few men have *Boss* answers.

No boss lies in the sun forever. The sun shines on a caporegime for a long time, but a boss must suffer. In the hereafter he lives forever; his name will never die, it is everlasting, ineradicable by space or time. But there is a price. No one wins endless smiles on Earth and then in the hereafter as well. *The life* offers alternate possibilities, a now and a hereafter. A caporegime will never know *Red Pepper*, but when he croaks, his name croaks too. In the end he is remembered by none. His life hasn't tilted *the life*. His birth was for nothing. History will not record a minute of his times or a mark of his being. If he has done good, the boss gets the credit. Better to be a boss, suffer *Red Pepper*, and have a name that lives on than to be a made guy who lived in the sun but only as an errand boy, and who, when dead, is forgotten. The caporegime gets a now; the boss gets a hereafter.

Too many aspire to *Boss* for *Red Pepper* not to come. When it does, a boss should be proud, for the gods bestow such troubles only on men of stature. Indeed, those troubles are alien to most. Onlookers will marvel at how the boss survives. They will say, "He is an old-timer, a man of the old country."

Red Pepper is when the law arrives at the boss's social club. Long cash is needed. Bail is high: $2 million. Lawyer fees are immense, millions more. Debts pile high. Dues tax the Family hard. Tough times follow.

The boss's lifetime of payola and building relationships, going all the way back to *Cooking Pot*—now is the time to call those people in. The boss has done many favors, so many favors are owed.

A war will brew. The boss will "have to go to the mattresses again, to get rid of some people," as Joe Valachi said. His most trusted men will turn enemy. They will come with kisses, but their kisses lie: they have no loyalty. To survive, the boss must be watchful. He will fight as long as he has the goodwill of the capos, but when the capos turn against him, he faces his destiny: if he wants to survive, he will have to step down and retire.

History

After Gotti organized the killing of Paul Castellano, Chin Gigante took to the mattresses, authorizing an attempt on Gotti's life. But when a car bomb went off outside the Veterans and Friends social club in Bensonhurst, Brooklyn, the man at the car door was not Gotti but his underboss, Frank DeCicco. Sammy Gravano rushed up and tried to pull DeCicco away. He would later recall, "I grabbed a leg, but he ain't coming with it. The leg is off. One of his arms is off. I got my hand under him and my hand went right through his body to his stomach. There's no ass. His ass, his balls, everything, is blown completely off. . . . I was wearing a white shirt. I looked at my shirt, amazed. There wasn't a drop of blood on it. The force of the blast, the concussion, blew most of the fluids out of Frankie's body. He had no blood left in him, nothing, not an ounce."

A few minutes earlier, as DeCicco walked toward his car with Lucchese Family soldier Frankie "Hearts" Bellino, he had noticed a bag underneath it. "Look at that bag. There's probably a bomb under my car," he had sarcastically told Hearts.

"CAR BOMB KILLS THE NO. 2 MAN IN CRIME FAMILY," was the headline on the front page of the *New York Times* on April 14, 1986. The article went on, "Federal and local law-enforcement officials said it was most likely that Mr. DeCicco was slain in retaliation for Mr. Castellano's murder."

After DeCicco's death, Gotti promoted Frank Locascio to underboss and Gravano to consigliere. The death of DeCicco, and increased legal scrutiny, did not sway Gotti from his in-your-face approach to leading the Gambino Family. He continued to hold court at the Ravenite in full sight of the law. Gravano and Locascio were required to report there five days a week and all twenty-one crew leaders had to report weekly. In Gravano's autobiography, *Underboss*, he noted that "some of the old foxes in the Family would come to me and say, 'Sammy, go talk to him—you're the only one who can get through to him. We got to stop this.' John's bringing every captain and every made guy in the Family down there. They'll see who kisses who, who talks to who, who gets the handshakes." But "the king insisted that the meetings be held in the throne room of his castle," wrote Gravano, so there the meetings were held. To Gotti, hiding in the shadows was a show of weakness. "Don't worry about it. You'll see—this will be okay. We're going to change the face of Cosa Nostra. We're going to show everybody how to do it. Everything will be good. I know what I'm doing. Fuck the government. They're nothing. Don't worry about it. You got to go in there with your suits, your jewelry. Put it in their face. When people go to the circus, they don't want to see clowns. They want to see fucking lions and tigers, and that's what we are."

"Okay," Gravano replied, "fuck the government. The boss is the boss. The boss's word is the final word."

Unbeknownst to Gotti, the feds were closing in. A wiretap in an apartment above the Ravenite recorded him voicing incriminating information, and on December 11, 1990, the full administration of the Gambino Family—Gotti, Gravano, and Locascio—were arrested at the club. Gotti was charged with murder, conspiracy to murder, loansharking, illegal gambling, obstruction of justice, bribery, and tax evasion. Held without bail, he pleaded not guilty.

Among other crimes, Gotti was overheard detailing the murders of capo Robert DiBernardo and soldier Louie DiBono. "I was in jail when I whacked him," Gotti said of DiBernardo. "I knew why it was being done. I done it anyway. I allowed it to be done anyway." Of DiBono Gotti said, "You know why he's dying? He's gonna die because he refused to come in when I called. He didn't do nothing else wrong."

Gotti was also overheard complaining to Locascio about Gravano, accusing him of selling out the Family for personal gain: "Every fuckin' time I turn around there's a new company popping up. Rebars, building, consulting, concrete. . . . I tell him a million times, 'Sammy, slow it down. Pull it in a fuckin' notch. You come up with fifteen companies, for Chrissake! You got rebars; you got concrete pouring; you got Italian floors now. You got construction; you got drywall; you got asbestos; you got rugs. What the fuck next?'" The tape was played back in court. Gravano heard it and fumed.

Gotti, Gravano, and Locascio—the administration of the Gambino Family—were being held without bail and were facing life without the possibility of parole. To keep the Family running, Gotti assembled a committee of his most trusted capos to carry out his orders: the Family would now be managed by his son Junior, his brother Pete, Lou Vallario, James "Jimmy Brown" Failla, and Jackie "Nose" D'Amico. "It was very easy at that time to get messages in and out" of the Metropolitan Correctional Center, where Gotti was held for trial, said Michael "Mikie Scars" DiLeonardo, capo in the Gambino family, in court testimony in 2006. Since "everything had to go through Junior before a decision was made or kicked up to his pop," Junior was effectively acting boss, DiLeonardo went on, but "he was told to stay in the background and keep the old-timers up front."

On November 13, 1991, Gotti's problems turned worse: Gravano, his underboss and most trusted friend, turned state's evidence. He would break the oath of omertà, testify against Gotti, and detail the inner workings of Cosa Nostra. The underworld was awed. Gravano was the first of his rank to turn—to switch governments. "He knew everything about everybody. He would send a lot of people to jail," said DiLeonardo.

Gravano was a loanshark on a grand scale: he had $1.5 million on the street. He also held a stranglehold over labor unions and construction contractors. After he turned informant, his rackets were given to DiLeonardo, who would manage the money and turn 50 percent of the profits over to Gotti. With DiLeonardo's newfound wealth came a warning from Jackie Nose and Pete Gotti: "If you screw up, we will kill you." For DiLeonardo, though, "The benefit was I was going to make a lot of money in the future."

Gravano's money was now DiLeonardo's money. In Cosa Nostra, your life and your money are not yours to keep. They are cloth of the Family. When leaving *the life*, you leave behind your life and your money. Life is a heartbeat, and the heartbeat of all things made is property of Cosa Nostra.

"We were not allowed to kill with bombs; we were not allowed to violate one another's wives or kids; we were not allowed to raise our hands to one another. John was the boss, I was underboss, and . . . Joe Piney was the consigliere. Frankie [Locascio] was acting consigliere," Gravano testified in 1992. He spilled everything: "There is the boss, the underboss, and the consigliere. It is the higher-up in the Family—the administration. A Commission is the Five Families in New York, the boss of every Family is a Commission. When you introduce one made member to another made member, you say 'he is a friend of ours' or '*amica nostra.*' If the guy is not a made member, you introduce him as 'a friend of mine.'"

Gravano also admitted to a role in nineteen murders, eight of them sanctioned by Gotti. Most notably he confessed to his role in the murder of Paul Castellano. His testimony assured Gotti's conviction.

In his memoir *Shadow of My Father*, published in 2015, Junior Gotti noted that "the flipping of Gravano had significant negative financial consequences for the Family. Fellows were afraid to collect monies, 'solicit' commissions on construction deals, everybody was afraid of exposure and arrest. This scenario made the maintaining of order within the Family more challenging." But Junior still had so much cash "he didn't know where to put it anymore," testified DiLeonardo. "John had nowhere to put any more of the cash. He was giving cash, large sums, to different guys around him to . . . be custodians on it." Junior took control of the money, "handled the lawyers; handled monetary issues," and "acted as eyes and ears" for his father, he said.

April 2, 1992, was judgment day. Gotti was facing the possibility of a life sentence. To influence the jury, he called in favors with his celebrity friends and asked some to be in the courtroom: the actors Mickey Rourke, Anthony Quinn, Al Lewis, and John Amos, the singer Jay Black of Jay and the Americans. But Gotti was found guilty on all charges and sentenced to life without the possibility of parole. "The Teflon is gone. The don is covered with Velcro, and all the charges stuck," said James Fox, director of the FBI office in New York.

Serving out his remaining days in the US penitentiary in Marion, Illinois, Gotti was confined to an eight-by-ten-foot prison cell for twenty-three hours a day. In 1996, he was assaulted by Walter Johnson, a black inmate. The fight ensued after Gotti directed a racial slur at Johnson, who pummeled Gotti, punching him repeatedly in the face. Bruised and beaten, Gotti was taken to the prison infirmary.

After many failed attempts to appeal his conviction, Gotti accepted his fate. "I've always felt in my heart that the day would come that my family and

I would be separated by prison." In a videotaped conversation with his daughter Vicky, he said, "Right now I'm cursed. I'm stuck in this joint here and that's the end of it." On June 10, 2002, ten years after his conviction, he died of throat cancer. He was sixty-one years old. He held on to power until his death: though not one of New York's other four Family bosses attended the funeral, hundreds of Gambino soldiers and capos showed up to pay respect to the "last don."

In one of Gotti's final conversations with Junior, he made clear that he would follow the code of Cosa Nostra until death. "When you go to war with me, I give no quarter and I ask for no quarter. When a man chooses a path, whether the choice be right or wrong, a man has to be true to himself, stay on that path, no matter how difficult it may be. When something is good, you can't say, 'This is for me,' but when it gets difficult, 'It's not.' Some decisions you make are for life. And a man, to be a man, stands by those decisions."

Reflection

Red Pepper is a boss's defining moment. It is his call to triumph or ruin. No matter the troubles—war, court, or coup—don't bet against a boss. Salvatore Maranzano triumphed in the Castellammarese War, fighting off the Joe Masseria faction from a mattress. In the mid-1960s, the Bonanno Family split in two and fought a civil war that the press dubbed the "Banana Split." Joe Bonanno's son Bill led the charge, fighting for his father's kingdom. Joe lost the war but did not yield to the Commission and was eventually allowed to retire.

The boss is primed for conflict. His body bears war wounds. Even in *Red Pepper*, he is a victor, for he's fighting a battle that few have fought. A lifetime of wins by a capo still ranks beneath every defeat of a boss. Even in defeat, a boss ranks with the greats, alive or dead.

As *Boss*, accept *Red Pepper*, however it comes. Survive it and you will feel the powers of capo di tutti capi, and your *Rosebush* will bear more buds than thorns.

EPOCH 5:
ROSEBUSH

Exposition

In *Rosebush*, all is made whole. The circle is squared. The boss has no advantage. Karma comes to the father. Retribution rules the day. In *Rosebush* the boss is killed or sentenced. He dies or loses his freedom.

For every gain sought and won in *the life*, *Rosebush* brings well-deserved grief. To rise from *Cooking Pot*, the boss created a protection racket. He not only offered protection, he carried out the beatings if the dues weren't paid. He lifted from the poor, hijacked cargo. As an up-and-comer, when called to from above he would take on a piece of work, murdering to order; he killed many men he did not know. To be made, the boss had to be an earner. He turned in millions to his godfather. He was trusted. He proved his loyalty to the men of honor. Maybe his father had brought him to America for a better life: rather than follow his father's teachings, he followed his godfather's teachings. He opted for a Lincoln and an apartment at the Waldorf.

As a soldier, the boss earned thousands; as a skipper, a caporegime, he earned millions. Much blood was poured; many businesses were cheated of their profit, extorted, bankrupted. The boss's strength graduated him from *Cooking Pot*, got him to *Made*, moved him to *Boss*, and earned him victory in *Red Pepper*. *Rosebush* is his final resting place.

The boss doesn't worry about the troubles of the soldier. For every day the boss enjoys, the soldier grieves. The soldier is a tool, a mamaluke. He has to bring the boss his money no matter what—or he dies. "Business bad? Fuck you, pay me. Oh, you had a fire? Fuck you, pay me. Place got hit by lightning, huh? Fuck you, pay me," as Hill explains in *Goodfellas*. Should the soldier's little daughter be starving, so be it: let her die. The boss must be paid.

The working man is an outsider, yet still a victim of the boss's greed. Cosa Nostra is a government and it taxes as such. *Fari vagnari a pizzu*: made or outsider, all men pay the *pizzo*, the protection money.

The soldier swore a blood oath to Cosa Nostra, the oath of omertà. So why does he live poor, owning not a dollar? Why does he get up in the morning and say "Son of a bitch, it's going to be a bad day"? Yet he still dresses in his best – topcoat, fedora – and goes about his work, even with nothing in his pocket. He does it because the boss's beak needs to be kept wet. In return, the one man the boss trusted, his friend since *Cooking Pot*, will have the boss killed and take his Family.

In Cosa Nostra there is no escape. Your options are limited: a boss must either die or grieve, for no boss becomes boss through good deeds. If a man has risen to *Boss*, he deserves grief, no matter how painful. Be it by the bullet or the prison, a boss suffers harsh pains in *Rosebush* as payment for his earthly gains.

A boss should not be cried for. Suppose the hitman sent for him misses his target and strikes the boss's daughter instead, and she is just a young girl: cry for her, but not for the boss. Every day of the boss's life, he has made humanity suffer. The death of a boss makes the world a better place. So don't cry for the boss who arrives at *Rosebush*. His pain is earned.

If a man wants to die in bed, he should not try for *Boss*. A boss dies in the street or in a cell. He doesn't live to spend the money he earned or to see his grandchildren mature. To die without a bullet or a cell is to cheat *the life* what it's owed. Peter Morello, Nick Terranova, Joe

Masseria, Toto D'Aquila, Manfredi Mineo, Frank Scalise, Vincent Mangano, Albert Anastasia, Paul Castellano, Joseph Pinzolo, Tom Reina, Joe Colombo, Salvatore Maranzano, and Carmine Galante all died by the bullet. John Gotti, Ducks Corallo, Carmine Tramunti, Vito Genovese, Vincent Gigante, Carmine Persico, and Philip Rastelli all died in prison. In Cosa Nostra, forget about it, the boss owes his life. "That is the rule," said Junior Gotti.

As Boss, don't plan on being Carlo Gambino or Frank Costello, Tom Gagliano or Tommy Lucchese, Joe Bonanno or Joe Profaci—all bosses who defied the odds and avoided paying the debt they owed. They died without having their body ripped by a tommy gun, without suffering the cold of the prison cell in which their bones were destined to rot. They have cheated *the life*. How dare a boss get out alive? This is not the rule of Cosa Nostra. They will burn in the next life.

No matter your wealth or stature, don't think you can shortchange *Rosebush*. If your goal is *Boss*, buy your cemetery plot now—for every boss earns retribution.

History

In 1976, Paul Castellano made Sammy Gravano. With his consigliere and underboss to his left and right and twenty-five caporegimes in a horseshoe around them, he told Gravano, "There is one way in and there is only one way out. You come in on your feet and you go out in a coffin." So Castellano knew the rules; he had been made in the Mangano Family in the 1940s. But according to Sammy Gravano, "Paul fucked up. He made a lot, a lot of mistakes." Gravano "thought the world of him in the beginning" but "he lost my love through a series of events. He lost the respect that Frankie DeCicco had for him. There was rumbling and growling by the troops. He changed from what he was in the beginning. He got more greedy. He just made one bad move after the other."

Born made—his father was a member of the Mangano Family—Castellano rose to *Boss* without the teachings of *Cooking Pot*. So he was ill prepared. Had he had *Cooking Pot* behind him, when he took over the Gambino Family after Carlo Gambino's death he would have killed Neil Dellacroce, John Gotti, and everyone loyal to Gotti. A *Cooking Pot Boss* does not dither with enemies. The boss who dithers is a *Made Boss*.

Castellano emphasized white rackets, such as construction and union bid-rigging. The blue-collar gangsters were left out. To the gangster a nickel is a nickel, be it from bootleg liquor or narcotics. A whiskey nickel and a junk nickel each spends as one nickel. So some of the blue-collar gangsters quietly sold heroin, which Castellano had banned.

Castellano built a mansion, the White House, in Todt Hill, Staten Island, where he lived like a god, removed from the soldiers. He shared his estate with both his wife, Nina, and his *gumada*, his mistress, Gloria Olarte. "He loved that fucking broad," said Gravano. For Gloria he would have killed his top-earning caporegime and soldier. Gravano: "The fifth Cadillac in the garage was Gloria's and Gloria dictated to his wife."

To Gravano and others in the family, Castellano was a fool for publicly humiliating his wife and children. "I lost a lot of respect for him. He had a gazillion dollars; he can get the most beautiful girl on the planet, buy her a house, buy her a Cadillac, make all the payments, go there every once in a while, do your little bullshit thing, and then go home," said Gravano. "She was two feet, fat, and ugly. What the fuck—and you expose your wife and kids and everybody in the house?"

Within both his own Family and the other four of the Five Families, Castellano had more foes than friends. He adamantly opposed drug dealing, a profitable racket for the soldiers, while walling himself off from them in a palace. He was greedy. He demanded more and more. He ruled by fear. He ate like a pig. "He normally spent four or five hours eating anything—the meat, the spaghettis, the vegetable, the coffee, the cake, the cookies. He never stopped," Olarte would remember. He was a glutton in money and in food.

The Castellano name traces back to the origins of the Sicilian Cosa Nostra, but Paul Castellano lacked the gangster instincts that are developed by growing up in poverty on the streets—by growing up in *Cooking Pot*. Gambino, a *Cooking Pot Boss*, had brought him along, but Paul was never called in to do a piece of work. He had no foundation in *Cooking Pot*; his foundation was in *Made*. When the Family needed to "throw a body in the street to wake these motherfuckers up," Michael DiLeonardo said, they called in men like John Gotti, not Paul Castellano. *Made* "is better than being a Hollywood star. You go to restaurants—you don't wait in line. They'll get you a table right away. You'll get the best of foods, the best of wines," according to Lucchese Family underboss Anthony "Gaspipe" Casso. But in *Cooking Pot* there's no food to eat, no wine to drink. Castellano was a *Made Boss*. He was unprepared to deal with men like Gotti.

On December 16, 1985, Castellano's newly appointed underboss, Tommy Bilotti, drove him to Sparks Steakhouse in Midtown Manhattan for dinner and a meeting with his capos. Gotti and Gravano sat in a parked car near the restaurant, Gravano holding a .357 Magnum. "As soon as Paul opened the car door, white jackets surrounded the car. They were shooting Paul. Tommy was watching Paul being shot. Part of the hit team was across the street. They came across and shot Tommy in the head—a bunch of times," Gravano would remember. Gotti and Gravano pulled up next to them and put the window down slightly: "He's gone," Gravano said.

Castellano once told Gloria Olarte, "I want to be happy. I want you to make me happy, because people like me die in the street."

Reflection

No boss escapes *Rosebush*. A boss should not depart *the life* unscathed. Retribution is a certainty. What will come will come.

The only people to escape *Rosebush* are common folk—outsiders and soldiers. A poor man may go free but never a boss, for he owes a debt of suffering. If you want to escape *Rosebush*, don't go for *Boss*. Collect garbage. Mop muck. Pour tar on a rooftop. Work until your hands are calloused and your back is arched. Be pissed on for all time. Or, choose *Boss*—and understand that if *Rosebush* isn't here now, it will come. Sooner or later, it will come. For all of us there is an end.

INTERLUDE:
THE BOSSES
AND MACHIAVELLI

"You might have heard that mob guys were into Machiavelli, a great Italian philosopher. His book is almost required reading for mob guys in prison. Mobsters believed the Machiavellian way of thinking would help them outsmart the next guy at a sit-down," writes Michael Franzese, formerly a caporegime in the Colombo Family. From its inception, Cosa Nostra used the teachings of the Renaissance diplomat Niccolò Machiavelli to gain and maintain power.

Salvatore Maranzano was known for his large library. He loved to discuss his readings and took a liking to Joe Bonanno, his mentee in America, since Bonanno, too, was learned in the history and principles of his heritage. Both men admired Machiavelli. "Among my Sicilian friends, in America, I was always singled out as a man of learning, if for no other reason than my ability to recite from *The Divine Comedy* or to expound on a few passages from *The Prince*," Bonanno wrote in his autobiography.

The Prince mattered in the underworld right through the time of the last don, John Gotti. Sammy "The Bull" Gravano, Gotti's friend and underboss, told the journalist Diane Sawyer, "A lot of members of the mob make it a point to read Machiavelli." The old-time bosses saw Machiavelli's teachings as their key to supremacy in the United States. Gotti in particular was known for his love of Machiavelli. He was picked up on FBI wiretaps quoting from *The Prince*. As a capo and boss, Gotti was known to direct his underlings through parables drawn from Machiavelli. "John was always quoting Machiavelli," said Gravano.

Gotti's predecessors Paul Castellano and Carlo Gambino urged their caporegimes to read *The Prince* as a go-to for understanding power. Author Selwyn Raab writes in his book *Five Families* that Gambino advised young recruits on "the philosophy that inspired his success"—"The lion frightens away the wolves. The fox recognizes traps. If you are like a lion and a fox, nothing will defeat you"—without telling them that he had lifted that philosophy from *The Prince*. Albert DeMeo, the son of Gambino Family capo Roy DeMeo, wrote in a memoir that "for his eleventh birthday, his mother bought him the Bible and his dad gave him a copy of Machiavelli's *The Prince*."

Most Cosa Nostra members were poorly schooled. Many never read a book in their life—except for *The Prince*, which was often the first and last book they opened. The few bookworms in Cosa Nostra might be mocked as lacking gangster qualities, but the bosses who controlled the largest footprint in their industry were often the well-studied ones. Meyer Lansky was a major contributor to the billion-dollar empire that Cosa Nostra became. "Meyer was always walking around with a book stuck in his back pocket and his nose buried in another one. The son of a bitch was always reading, always learning something," said Charlie "Lucky" Luciano.

Cosa Nostra men from soldier to boss were influenced by Machiavelli, some knowingly, many unknowingly. Teachings, traditions, and rules of attaining power that they adhered to staunchly were derived from *The Prince*, passed down to them through the Family whether or not they ever read the book. As Italians lined up to board boats for their new country, they brought with them, embedded in their psyches, the teachings of Machiavelli.

Niccolò di Bernardo dei Machiavelli was born in Florence on May 3, 1469. His father, Bernardo, a lawyer, had his son well educated and provided him with books for his personal study. Niccolò grew up during the Renaissance, a period of great social change and of radical developments in philosophy, soldiery, art, politics, and literature. When he was young, Florence was ruled by the Medici family, who, however, lost power in 1487. The city now became a republic, and here Machiavelli prospered, advancing to a significant government position by the time he was thirty.

In 1512, Giovanni de Medici seized power, returning the republic to Medici rule. Machiavelli was removed from his post and arrested for conspiracy. Released after being tortured for three weeks, he retired to his estate, where he would research and write *The Prince*. Describing the book as the greatest gift that he had to offer, he dedicated it to Lorenzo de Medici, Giovanni's cousin, whom Giovanni had installed in power in Florence in 1513 after he himself became pope:

> Those who strive to obtain the good graces of a prince are accustomed to come before him with such things as they hold most precious, or in which they see him take most delight; whence one often sees horses, arms, cloth of gold, precious stones, and similar ornaments presented to princes, worthy of their greatness. Desiring therefore to present myself to your Magnificence with some testimony of my devotion towards you, I have not found among my possessions anything which I hold more dear than, or value so much as, the knowledge of the actions of great men, acquired by long experience in contemporary affairs, and a continual study of antiquity; which, having reflected upon it with great and prolonged diligence, I now send, digested into a little volume, to your Magnificence.

The Prince went unpublished in Machiavelli's lifetime. There is no evidence to suggest that Lorenzo ever read it. It waited to appear in print until 1532, nineteen years after it was written and five years after Machiavelli's death.

Machiavelli's treatise became a centerpiece of Italian thought and significantly influenced the establishment of Cosa Nostra. As Franzese says,

> Machiavelli was kind of the patron saint of the mob. When you went into prison it was almost required that you read *The Prince*. And just to explain, in *The Prince*, Machiavelli is supposed to consult or guide the prince and give him guiding principles on how to maintain control of his country; of his leadership. And one of the main principles was this: he told the prince that you can do anything that you need to do—you can lie; you can steal; you can cheat; you can kill—you can do anything you need to do to maintain power. Because that's the major goal: maintain power and control over your kingdom. But in doing so you must always appear to the outside person to be upright, to have integrity, and to be honest. And that's the Machiavellian way—the end justifies the means, anything goes—but you have to appear to be upright, honest, and have integrity. And to a large degree, with certain things, that's how the mob operated: we got what we wanted; the end justifies the means as long as we get what we want in the end. But we're supposed to do it in a way that shows that we have honor and integrity and honesty among one another. So that's it. Now, is that a good way to live? Of course not. Because it has no restrictions on you. As a matter of fact, Machiavelli says, "It's better for you to have no restrictions on you because then you can do anything that you want as long as you appear to have restrictions on you—morally." So, is it a good way to live? Of course not. Because anything goes. You can lie, you can steal, you can cheat, you can do anything that you want in order to maintain control and to get what you want. So, obviously it's not a good way to live and in the end, you're going to fail as a result.

RULE
1

USE A SKILLED MAN
TO YOUR BENEFIT

A Prince… should honour those who excel in every art.
He… should provide rewards… for all who are disposed in any way
to add to the greatness of his City or State.

—Niccolò Machiavelli, *The Prince*, 1513

RULE 1:
USE A SKILLED MAN TO YOUR BENEFIT

I didn't have to love him to use him.

—Charlie "Lucky" Luciano

A boss who is unwilling to adapt to new ideas is a Mustache Pete. The Petes are set in their ways, liking the Family as it stands: familiar in its Sicilianness, but stagnant. If a Family of five soldiers and a caporegime all come from Sicily, a Pete will consider it pure, rejecting criminals of other nationalities even if they're good earners. Because the Mustache Petes' old ways of doing things will not advance the Family into the future, they should be killed or put on the shelf.

As boss, judge a man not by his heritage but by his skill. Your Family needs earners, whether or not they are pure-blooded Sicilians. **Truth: Unless you increase profits for the Family, you have no value to the Family.** If everyone in your crew comes from Sicily but a smart Jew has a good stock market scheme and a connection to rig bids in the construction business, welcome said Jew into the Family. **Truth: Dollars in the hands of white people, Black people, red people, blue people, or purple people, they're still green, and they spend.**

Try as you may—search the saloons, the speaks, the brothels, the carpet joints—a skilled soldier is hard to find. So ignore a man's ethnicity. If four assassins stand left of a lone Jew as he looks right and yet the Jew survives, drawing his pistol and killing all four, then he is skilled with guns: make him your hit man. If he is wise in books, keeps up with current events, studies the political landscape, and knows math, make him your consigliere. Measure a man by his potential to earn and your tenure as boss will be long.

No boss is so capable as to have no need of a skilled team. Fill a Family with men of more talent than you have and your Family will be harder to attack. As boss, never worry about being outshone; having a talented man in your crew is to your benefit. Make him a made man. He will be a fine soldier. **Truth: A skilled man's skill becomes your skill when you hire him.**

RULE
2

BEWARE OF THE KISS

It is customary for such as seek a Prince's favour, to present themselves before him with those things of theirs which they themselves most value, or in which they perceive him chiefly to delight.

—Niccolò Machiavelli, *The Prince*, 1513

RULE 2:
BEWARE OF THE KISS

If a guy brings you a basket, it don't make him a good guy. It makes him a motherfucker to me. It don't make him a good guy. It makes him a good guy when he's one of us.

—John Gotti

The boss and all men beneath him, down to the lowly associates, are motivated by dollars. In matters of the dollar, the boss and the soldier align.

A soldier warms to a boss's affection. **Truth: Sincerity and bosses are not one.** The bosses of the Five Families did not rise to power through compassion. If you are a boss, you have swindled and cheated your way up. You deceived your friends. You skimmed off the top before the profits were split, ending up with a higher percentage than you were owed. **Truth: If your boss plays noble, your boss is a liar, for no boss is ruled by nobility.**

The same boss to whom you have sworn omertà will authorize your death with a kiss. You may have worked with distinction, but don't be silly enough to think the boss will protect your interests. The boss follows power and dollars. He feels no affection for you—what he feels affection for is the percentage you turn in. If he requires 10 percent, don't try to turn in 9. If 9 sufficed, 9 would have been set; it was not.

The boss and the soldier are alike in their taste for misdirection. **Truth: When an enemy is preparing to strike, he will come bearing gifts and an envelope full of cash. Before he leaves, he**

will kiss you on both cheeks. When you are boss, receive a kiss with caution. Even in moments of apparent nobility and generosity, your soldier cannot be trusted.

Truth: If two fish can satisfy your hunger, you will hook three. And if a bucket holds four fish, and two hungry people stand in front of it, the first person to reach it will take all four fish. So be wary. A smiling man is a devious man, for a smile is welcomed while a frown is turned away. How will a frowning man kill you? Won't his frown make you move to defend yourself? If you want someone to lower his guard, smile, then kill him. **Truth: Kiss a man and he will kiss you in return.** So if someone comes with a kiss, he has come to kill you. Beat him until his heart stops.

Whether talking to a rival or a friend, a boss will be polite, for the relaxed are easier to kill than the angry. So if a ranking man laughs at your jokes and compliments your shoes, you may be in the company of an assassin. When you turn your back, the shell from a double-barrel sawed-off will exit your front.

Truth: "Everybody has larceny in them," as Lucky Luciano said. Everyone is suspect. But they can make their words riddle and dance, dressing up their dialogue to relax you. So if a man brings you a basket full of goodies, kill him. You have something that he wants—kill him, for he has come to collect a corpse. He has dug and limed a hole to fit your body. Waste no time: kill him quickly and bury him in the hole that he has made for you. **Truth: If a man sleeps in the bed he has made, why shouldn't he be buried in the hole he has dug?**

RULE
3
STEP DOWN, RETIRE

When men attempt things within their power, they will always be praised rather than blamed. But when they persist in attempts that are beyond their power, mishaps and blame ensue.

—Niccolò Machiavelli, *The Prince*, 1513

RULE 3:
STEP DOWN, RETIRE
Know when your time is up.

Right now I'm cursed. I'm stuck in prison and that's the end of it.

—John Gotti

Suppose your coffers are stuffed with cash and your name will live on. Why grace the Family longer? **Truth: A soldier works his rackets to turn dollars for the day but a boss works to turn dollars for tomorrow.** Isn't the goal to be rich and revered? Don't all men, boss and soldier alike, want the night to end and the morning to come? Doesn't a man want to live to be gray, working in the garden, clipping the roses, remembered as "the Prime Minister of the Underworld," like Frank Costello? **Truth: A man works when he is young, risking his life and saving his money, in the hope that his old age will be plush.**

As boss, head the Family for as long as you are valued and still leading from a position of strength. If the Commission still honors your vote and your caporegimes and soldiers still shoot at your order, your time has yet to expire. But if the soldiers are breaking the rules and the caporegimes are getting killed, your doom is imminent. A tommy gun will rip open your chest or a double-barrel will shatter your skull, priming you for the customary closed-casket funeral.

You are rich. You have an apartment in the Majestic on Central Park West and a mansion on Staten Island. Your wife lives high and your mistress does too. You have interests in rackets spreading west to east and your offshore holdings are sizable. So why keep leading the Family?

You've done it for north of two decades. The administrations of all Five Families have sought your counsel. As for cash, you're sitting on a bundle that will feed the next three generations of your kin. What more do you have to gain? **Truth: Once you have pocketed the money, the power, and the respect, you should step down and retire.** A man should not outstay his welcome. Ignore this rule and cheers will become boos, partners will become enemies, and affection will turn to disdain.

The higher a boss rises, the higher the expectation. You will be asked for even more spectacular results, doubling the profits and deepening the Family footprint. So once you have led the Family to new heights, don't make a second attempt. Step down and retire, like Frank Costello. Call a meeting with the heads of the Five Families and ask to vacate your post. In gratitude for your good work and decades of service, the bosses will oblige. You will be permitted to retain your interest and hold court at the Majestic, advising Tommy Lucchese and Don Carlo Gambino.

Truth: Lose the respect of your Family and your public and you will not regain it. Try as you may—pray to God in heaven or drop on bent knee to the Commission—all will prove futile. A boss is the boss once. Should he fall from that topmost post and try to regain it, he will forever be chasing the ghost of his former self. Once a boss has been replaced, he will never lead a Family again.

RULE
4

KISS THE RING

Thinking it beneath him to serve under others… he formed the design to seize on that town…. And it would have been impossible to unseat him… had he not let himself be overreached by Cesare Borgia, who took him with the Orsini and Vitelli at Sinigaglia. Thus he was strangled.

—Niccolò Machiavelli, *The Prince*, 1513

RULE 4:
KISS THE RING
The boss is the boss.

Obedience to one's superiors was one of the duties of a Family member.

—Joe Bonanno

A boss distrusts his soldiers, for every soldier, green or seasoned, dreams of leading the Family. Envying his boss's influence and wealth, he waits for the moment when he can rob the boss of his throne. **Truth: A man does not rise by being complacent.** Every boss spends his green days as a soldier—how does he become a boss? **Truth: The boss is the boss because he killed his boss.**

As a soldier, know that your boss doesn't trust you. Look humble, keep your ears open wider than your mouth, and obey the boss's decrees. Oblige him and earn his trust.

Truth: If you run a loan book or numbers racket, your boss ran those rackets too. If you supply the speaks and carpet joints, your boss too supplied the speaks and carpet joints. If you have killed five men, your boss has killed ten. So don't envy your boss as he is chauffeured in a Lincoln, don't envy him taking tête-à-têtes at the barbershop, don't envy him drinking vino in the Copacabana. Your boss lugged mattresses in the thick of the Castellammarese War. He paid cash for the politicians and judges you have inherited free of charge. For the work your boss has done, kiss his ring in gratitude. Whether in war or peace, give him his due: your trigger finger, a percentage of your rackets, and your respect.

Like every boss, when you're coming up you will work the streets—hijacking, bootlegging, executing the boss's orders. You will war with your counterpart soldiers in rival factions. Your caporegime will disrespect you and exacting tasks will be demanded of you. You will be badly paid, you will clock long hours, your bathroom will be the alley, you'll skip lunch because you have not a nickel in your pocket, and just when you think you have satisfied the boss and promotion is imminent, you will be demoted. Your green days will be painful. **Truth: A time will come when you are called in to make your bones.** You will be asked if you are ready to kill. You will be given a brown-paper bag. Inside will be a revolver. You will be ordered to murder a man you do not know. You must kill whoever you are asked to, and you must not fail, for the wisest and richest boss was once a low-ranked associate who was sent out on a piece of work "on record"—on orders from the boss.

Truth: To be a boss, you must first work under a boss.
The most cunning and ruthless boss was once a soldier without power or respect, a flunky taking orders from a caporegime and fetching like an errand boy, working high-risk low-reward rackets. If you're a soldier, don't imagine you're ready for leadership without first being an apprentice, as even the capo di tutti capi once was. On your rise, run get your boss's cannoli. Make his coffee hot and to his liking. If he steps out of a Lincoln in the rain, stand by his side with an umbrella. If he's cold, drape him in an overcoat. When he speaks, listen. Observe. Watch his gait. How does he receive underlings? How does he conduct himself with another boss—does his speech slow while his ears open, or do his ears shut while his tongue dances? **Truth: Mimic your boss.** Don't advise, be advised. You are a student—be a student.

Truth: There is no god but the boss. If the boss says go, go; if he says stay, stay. The boss comes first—he is the only thing in your life. You do everything with the boss. You check with the boss, you put everything on record with the boss. You can't do anything on your own initiative. You can't pull a trigger or aim a gunsight without permission from the boss.

If you can't submit to your boss, accepting him as your teacher, you are unfit to lead the Family. Promotion will elude you—you will stay a soldier running meager rackets and performing mundane tasks until the day when you are shot and stuffed in a barrel.

To prime yourself for leadership, devote your green days to the painful, labor-intensive work handed down by the boss. Be Joe Bonanno: "a squire in the service of a knight." Do that and you will be accepted in Cosa Nostra. Do not, and you will never rise in rank. As your old age comes near, you will wonder whether it was worth it to dedicate your life to the Family. You will be destitute while the boss you served for decades is a millionaire. If you have managed to become a caporegime, your tenure will be short and your fall will be more painful than your climb. The feds will infiltrate your crew, the IRS will seize your savings, the media will savage you, and your partners will turn away. All you have worked for will be no more.

What will ready you for leadership is the rules, traditions, and values taught to you by your boss. So serve him well. Be alert in his presence. Meet his every demand. Soak up his teachings and morals and absorb his strengths. Learn to appreciate his presence and his years of experience.

But once you have acquired your boss's skills in leading the caporegimes, established your own rapport with his contacts in City Hall, and assured the police commissioner and his captains that their grease will continue, you need your boss no more. That need is annulled. Once your mentor and father, he is now an impediment, and what impedes you must be removed. So shoot him five times as he reclines for a shave in the Park Sheraton Hotel. If he raises his left arm in defense, shoot his hand, shoot his wrist, shoot his left hip, and shoot him twice more, once in the back and once in the head. Don Umberto "Albert" Anastasia will be no more.

RULE

5

MIX WITH
THE SOLDIERS

When you are on the spot, disorders are detected in their beginnings and remedies can be readily applied; but when you are at a distance, they are not heard of until they have gathered strength and the case is past cure.

—Niccolò Machiavelli, *The Prince*, 1513

RULE 5:
MIX WITH THE SOLDIERS
Keep a pulse on your operation.

I started to organize his whole fucked-up operation. It was a lot of business to tie up right, but in about six months, I had it all running smooth as silk.

—Charlie "Lucky" Luciano

Because the soldier's rank is petty, he watches his petty rackets and his petty profits vigilantly. His concern is survival—earning enough to stay afloat without breaking a rule that could get him killed. But thinking only about himself disengages him from his Family. He has nothing, but out of his nothing he has to give his capo something; stuck in a rat wheel, he grows isolated, engulfed in his problems. His vision of the world around him blurs and he only sees the reality of himself. This makes the soldier a threat to the boss because he can easily be bribed. So, as boss, think broadly about the whole *borgata* and don't shield yourself from the Family you lead. Stay away from the streets that feed your soldiers and your influence will wane and the Family will implode, inviting civil war and leaving you vulnerable.

When you are boss, nothing—from a penny slot to a whore's legs—should move without your knowing. You have to keep your finger on the pulse of the Family. Tell your underboss to call a sit-down for the caporegimes where they will report on what they are involved in and how much they are earning. A dollar cannot go uncounted and a whisper cannot fall on deaf ears. If you are out of the caporegimes' eye, they will support whoever rises against you. **Truth: Absence generates defectors.** If your followers don't feel led, they will go astray. As sure as a made guy lives and dies by the gun, lead from a distance and the caporegimes will plot to oust you. An adviser you trust will turn against you, organizing a meeting where you will be killed.

Truth: Your caporegimes meet in your absence. Seeing you as weak and inattentive, they take the pulse of the old-timers and top soldiers in their Family and of friends in the other four. Soldiers are weak and the weak need leaders. Fail to lead and your soldiers will realign, throwing their muscle behind the caporegime who wants *Boss*.

Truth: The Family is all important. Remember the oath: your son may have no more than an hour to live, but if the Family calls, you have to leave him. If your daughter is ill in the wee hours and the Family calls, leave her to her coughing. Nothing takes priority over *this thing of ours*. Even for the boss, Cosa Nostra comes first, no matter what. So stay connected. Only by being present can you detect discontent in the ranks. The Family is too valuable to be left unguarded.

Truth: A boss is only as strong as his soldiers are loyal. Power lies in numbers, weakness in isolation. If your soldiers rebel, you will die. Try as you may, once they revolt you cannot reverse them—take what you can and step down.

RULE

6

INVEST TOTALLY

A Prince must lay solid foundations, since otherwise he will inevitably be destroyed.

—Niccolò Machiavelli, *The Prince*, 1513

RULE 6:
INVEST TOTALLY
Die by the rules you live by.

Everybody makes himself inconspicuous when the captain asks for volunteers for night patrol. But one man, the pure warrior, has already rubbed burnt cork on his face. He believes winning the war is his personal responsibility.

—Joe Bonanno

When the pantry is empty and the schoolbooks provide no solution, what does a boy do? Since he can't earn in high school, a future boss works the streets, armed with a pistol and leading a trusted gang. He knows that the streets harbor dollars and that dollars buy food. Instead of graduating high school he graduates from the school of hard knocks. Once you have sworn omertà and vowed to the saints that you will live and die by the gun and the knife, you have to own it.

Your chosen path will be dangerous, bringing out your worst fears and frustrations. But on your rise to boss, you can't be put off by the difficulties of *the life*. If you want to rule the Family, accept the fight.

Truth: Where a boss is fearless, a soldier is cautious. Build a barrier before a boss and he will jump over it. Stand a soldier there and he will lose nerve, wonder what's waiting on the other side, and eventually turn around, returning to the world that so pains him. The next day he will get back on his feet only to cower once more.

The soldier's domain is the alley. He will never live at the Waldorf. But the boss is a boss. His footprint stretches from New York to Italy. Having chosen a life in *the life*, he invests totally.

Be it noble or ignoble, the path you choose should get your best effort. If you hijack cargo, your score should be Lufthansa (the 1978 heist that netted almost $6 million—worth almost $27 million in the dollars of the early 2020s). If you are a labor racketeer, get Jimmy Hoffa and his Teamsters in your pocket. Invest just a half and your take will be a half; instead, plant both feet. **Truth: If the rackets bring you life, be ready for the rackets to bring you death.** To be a man of honor, you must be prepared to suffer and die, for that is the only path to *Boss*. And once you have reached that peak, stand before your soldiers and tell them that you are God, the boss of bosses—that no man comes close to your glory, or ever will.

RULE

7

BE VIGILANT
OF YOUR RIVALS

They are thinking more of themselves than of you, and against such men a Prince should be on his guard, and treat them as though they were declared enemies.

—Niccolò Machiavelli, *The Prince*, 1513

RULE 7:
BE VIGILANT OF YOUR RIVALS

We have to go to the mattress again. We have to get rid of these people.

—Salvatore Maranzano

A boss cannot be distracted by success. Maybe your rackets are booming and the elites are begging to consult you—don't let them entice you into relaxing your focus.

As a soldier, you were vigilant and skeptical. You moved as warily as a cat, distrusting your public and your government. Now that you're boss, the Commission may yield to your demands, millions of dollars may be coming in, the governor's office may be on your payroll—but don't think your Family is bulletproof. Respectability, influence, and cash don't make you invulnerable. The bullet that kills the soldier will kill the boss. Despite your *Time*-magazine cover, your news clippings, your construction racket, despite the three federal indictments that failed to find you guilty, you must know when your enemy is near.

Glitz and glamour make a soldier lower his guard, make him loose with his tongue and blind to the world. He will dance at the disco and sniff of the powder. He will drink wine in excess and lose on the horses. Ruin will surely ensue. **Truth: When the soldier's pockets are bulging, he is destructive.** His success is temporary and his death is near.

Shine bright and your glow will be seen. You are desired by the most beautiful women. You have safe-deposit boxes in Zurich. A three-piece suit, quality loafers, a chauffeured Lincoln, acquittals in court—you are picture perfect, and what is photo friendly lures lights and lenses. Imagine yourself called the Teflon Don, as John Gotti was, and hailed as the messiah by the public and the press. But the messiah you are not. You are a boss. Ignore the flattery of the public and the media: in the morning when you wake and at night when you sleep, ten enemies are dreaming of your doom.

Once you reach the pinnacle of the Family, your enemies embrace you and laugh at your jokes. Every idea you propose is accepted without argument. But don't be fooled: there is an assassin nearby, aiming at your head. **Truth: Your enemy stands before you at dusk; your enemy stands before you at dawn.** He runs your errands, speaks on your behalf. Who is your enemy? Look to your right: it is your underboss, your topmost friend. **Truth: Your enemy is he who sits closest to you.** He whom you most trust. When the hammer comes down, don't look to your soldiers for the culprit; the man behind the gun will be your underboss, your second-in-command, your most senior adviser. It is he who is your enemy.

Truth: To be boss is to be betrayed and die.

Envelopes full of cash, abundant women, and endorsements from ranking men will make you feel untouchable. But nothing is permanent. What you see today will change tomorrow. So don't be fooled by the beauty of the moment: when the streets are quiet and the coast seems clear, your house is under siege and your enemy is closing in on you.

RULE
8

BREAK THE RULES

Soldiers rushing out from places of concealment put Giovanni and all the rest to death. After this butchery, Oliverotto mounted his horse, rode through the streets, and besieged the chief magistrate in the palace, so that all were constrained by fear to yield obedience and accept a government of which he made himself the head. And all who from being disaffected were likely to stand in his way, he put to death.

—Niccolò Machiavelli, *The Prince*, 1513

RULE 8:
BREAK THE RULES

The minute I get out, I'm killing this motherfucker.

—Frank Locascio

In *the life*, the boss calls his underlings to the carpet to lay down the Family rules. "If you break rules, you end up in a dumpster," said Junior Gotti. But the rules are written to protect the interests of the boss. The boss will say that the rules are strict to ensure the longevity of the Family. **Truth: The rules are drawn and enforced to protect the interests of authority (the boss) while disenfranchising the commoner (the soldier).** So don't subscribe to your boss's rhetoric, for even he, the topmost authority, will sacrifice honor to his own interests.

A soldier cannot so much as extend a handshake to the boss. If gratitude is to be expressed, it is on the boss's initiative. For the soldier, the boss is unapproachable. Suppose the problem is serious and your caporegime is no help, you reach the boss through an intermediary, the consigliere. You have no access to the boss. He is off in his mansion, indifferent to your needs and unsympathetic to your worries.

To make the Family work for you, you must break the rules. Your boss must die. How long will you let him dine off your rackets? How long will you kill men you have no bad feeling for on his behalf? How long will you duck and hide from the law, maybe waste years in Dannemora, and be called to the carpet for violations you did not commit? **Truth: If you have been a soldier for two decades, you have suffered for two decades.** Until you break the rules, your pain will persist.

Breaking the rules means disrupting the Family order. As order dies, so will the boss's power. **Truth: The road that leads to Boss is a high-risk road.** Without risk there is no reward. To rule the Family you must break the rules you have sworn to obey. Unless you break the rules, you will never rise to the top of the Family.

Truth: A boss will eliminate anyone who threatens the Family. If you're found breaking a rule, the boss will quickly have you killed. He will do it without hesitation, guilt, or fear of retribution, for a soldier is insignificant. He will kill you without a second thought.

There is just one path to leading the Family: breaking the boss's rules, and doing it undetected. As you break the rules—selling narcotics, say, or killing made men—be sure not to challenge the boss. Otherwise your end will come fast. Sleep with another member's wife, kill without permission, and sell drugs all over New York, but you must somehow stay spit-shine clean in the eyes of your boss.

If you can't break the rules, you will never be seated anywhere but at a table of soldiers. To rule the Family you must first rise in rank, for a soldier rarely speaks to the boss. **Truth: Bosses talk not to soldiers but to the rich and influential.** So you must rise, first to caporegime, then to underboss. To do that, break the rules.

Rules are laid down to keep order. Bosses like order; without it, soldiers would govern themselves. Without order, everything strong is weakened, everything advancing falls back, everything abundant grows scarce. But you can't generate disorder as a soldier; you must rise into the leadership, at least to caporegime, for a soldier's troublemaking will be brought to an end long before it troubles the boss. Once you have risen into the hierarchy, you will be close enough to the boss to kill him. Take over the Family, rewrite the rules, and make them even stricter than your predecessor did, for now you must protect yourself. A young soldier is rising in the Family. He wants to be boss, and one day he will be.

RULE
9

DRESS DAPPER

When evening comes, I go back home, and go to my study. On the threshold, I take off my work clothes, covered in mud and dirt, and I put on the clothes an ambassador would wear. Decently dressed, I enter the ancient courts of rulers who have long since died. There, I am warmly welcomed.... I am not ashamed to talk to them and ask them to explain their actions and they, out of kindness, answer me.

—Niccolò Machiavelli, *The Prince*, 1513

RULE 9:
DRESS DAPPER

*I had on a beautiful double-breasted dark oxford gray suit, a plain
white shirt, a dark blue silk tie with little tiny horseshoes on it....
I had a charcoal-gray herringbone cashmere topcoat, because it was
a little cool, with a Cavanagh gray fedora.*

—Charlie "Lucky" Luciano

A boss who dresses to the nines will act with sophistication, exerting
a confidence and charm denied to those wearing casual clothes. He
dresses formally because he knows that at a moment's notice he may be
summoned to a meeting with men of his ilk. **Truth: The dapper man
is looked on not with scorn but with envy.**

Where a soldier works his rackets in denim, the boss has "somebody
picking out his clothes," as Sammy Gravano said of John Gotti. The
boss is the boss. Gotti wore three-piece suits tailored by Brioni.
He had "a couple dozen suits, sports jackets, all kinds of shirts and
turtlenecks, ties, shoes all shined up, socks, and a hankie for his coat
pocket." His car was a Mercedes. It was washed and cleaned every
day. "Not even a speck can be on or in the car," said Gravano. So
shave immaculately, wear unmatchable clothes, and the boss will see
you as worthy of promotion. Show up whiskered and dirty and you
will work in the brothels with the barkeeps until you die.

No matter the occasion, dress sharp. So the meeting is held in an
alley reeking of urine, and the attendees are madams and pimps:
stand in that foulness as if it were the Atlantic City Conference of

1929. Nothing can put a dent in your appearance. Otherwise you will be seen as a mere friend of mine, rather than a friend of ours. **Truth: Appear as a soldier and a soldier you will be.**

RULE
10
KILL THE BOSS

He who conspires always reckons on pleasing the people by putting the Prince to death.

—Niccolò Machiavelli, *The Prince*, 1513

RULE 10:
KILL THE BOSS

When you become boss in this life, you don't get elected.
You eliminate the boss above you.

—Michael Franzese

Truth: Nothing is sacred.

If you are at odds with your boss, he will plot against you and soon
you will be no more. Once he has marked you out, no reversal is
possible. Death will find you. So don't cower: pick up your gun.
Truth: A soldier dies on his knees; a boss dies on the mattresses.

Your boss won't be easy to kill. On the day, dress for death, because if
you miss, it will be over before you get a second shot. You will be made
an example and your death will be hard: maybe your hands will be
chopped off, your tongue cut out, your throat slit, your penis severed
and shoved into your throat, and, after you have suffered immensely,
your limbs and head removed, stuffed into a barrel of cement, and
sunk in the East River. You will get no proper burial, your remains
will never be recovered, and your family will wonder for a lifetime
where you are, unsure whether you're dead or alive, unsure how to
mourn.

Truth: Your boss is "a fish on the desert... a fish out of water.
He don't know this life," as John Gotti said of Paul Castellano. He
is long tenured and long tenure makes a man arrogant. His decades
of unopposed leadership have blurred his vision. Drinking vino
and eating pasta, he has grown fat and lazy. He is distant from the

streets. He is not a gangster, he is a racketeer. He meets with the Commission, he reads the *Wall Street Journal*, he talks not with the soldiers but with the bosses. He is complacent and out of touch, and he must go.

As you rise in the Family, being promoted from associate to soldier, from soldier to caporegime, your growth will be stymied once you reach the next rank, the second-most senior in the administration: underboss. Your final promotion, from underboss to boss, you will only achieve by yourself. The boss who has guided you for north of a decade, who has made you and made you rich, teaching you the rackets and promoting you within the Family, must now die. Otherwise you will never be boss.

Truth: Everything Frank Costello knew, he stole. Haven't you stolen your boss's knowledge of the rackets and his contacts in government? Haven't you adopted his cunning in acquiring new rackets and eliminating rival factions? Haven't you modeled yourself on his cold persona and his loose sense of honor and loyalty? **Truth: You have worked the streets for the boss; you have murdered by the dozen for him.** Your nights on the mattresses, the scar across your face—they have come to you through the boss and your affection for his Family. So every bullet you pump into the boss is deserved. He has earned every shot. Blood must spout from his face, knives must pierce his chest, his throat must be slashed ear to ear. As he gasps a last breath and then lies dead, your tailored clothes should be sodden with blood—if not, you missed a spot. If you are to move up in the Family, your boss must die. **Truth: A boss will not surrender his Family; his power must be usurped.** And then he must die—let him live and he will avenge himself later.

Once you have risen in wealth and influence, your boss will start to worry that you are becoming too powerful. You must seem to submit to him fully, demonstrating your subservience. **Truth: Before your** boss rose to *Boss*, he was an underboss like you. So he knows how you think. He knows you want to run the Family. He is constantly taking your pulse to see whether or not you are a threat. If he thinks you are, he will oust you with a bullet.

An underboss, though, is not so easily removed. He is powerful and influential, in becoming underboss he has won respect from the caporegimes and the soldiers, and he has contacts in the legislature and the police force. And if a boss attacks his underboss without cause, the Family will split, some aligning with the boss, some with the underboss. The Family will be at war.

So a boss will not move against an underboss as quickly as he would against a soldier. As the underboss grows stronger, the boss has two options: align with the underboss or kill him. If the underboss keeps working the union locals, attending meetings when called in, and turning in $2 million a year, the boss will spare his life. But if the boss sees the underboss as a threat, he will kill him. **Truth: If your boss has marked you as a threat but still seems to be trying to align with you, he is buying time.** He is plotting against you, working to weaken you—stealing your resources and ordering hits against those loyal to you. Once your power has waned and your loyalists sleep with the fishes, he will eliminate you.

Truth: A boss cannot be trusted. If you're ever at odds with him, you have just one option: act fast and kill him or he will beat you to it. Should the boss feel threatened, he won't hold a sit-down or give you a chance to explain. He will put a hole in your head. If given the opportunity, you must do the same.

Truth: If you are to rule the Family, its boss must die. If you're not willing to kill him, you're not fit for leadership. Every boss, whether his tenure is long or short, has risked death before rising to *Boss*. **Truth: The price of *Boss* is your life.** If you're not ready to pay that price, you will stay a soldier. What separates the boss from the soldier is fearlessness. Whether on the lam, hiding out from a team of assassins, facing fifty years in Dannemora, or threatened with the chair, a boss is fearless.

To be a boss, you will have to fight a boss. The boss you served honorably and effectively will be the boss you have to fight. If you are an associate, your boss—the soldier who mentored and guided you—must die if you are to take his place. If you are a soldier, your boss—the caporegime who mentored and guided you—must die if you are to take his place. If you are a caporegime, your boss—the underboss who mentored and guided you—must die if you are to take his place. If you are an underboss, your boss—the boss who mentored and guided you—must die if you are to take his place and lead the Family. You cannot lead the Family on bent knee. Go to the mattresses, and as Sammy "The Bull" Gravano instructed the hit team on the Castellano murder, "If it means you have to die there, then die there. Die there in a gun battle with the cops—but do not back off of this hit." If you must die, die with your guns drawn. Better to die standing up than to live sitting down.

And when you kill your boss, do it honorably: shoot him in the face when his eyes are open.

RULE
11

ACCEPT RISK

*The difficulties that attend conspirators are infinite, and we know
from experience that while there have been many conspiracies,
few of them have succeeded.*

—Niccolò Machiavelli, *The Prince*, 1513

RULE 11:
ACCEPT RISK

If I get fifty years, I know what I got to do.

—John Gotti

The Commission bosses have been abundantly rewarded. Their wealth will last a day past forever, they have pull in every high office in the state, and they have shaken hands with Herbert Hoover, Franklin D. Roosevelt, Benito Mussolini, and Fulgencio Batista. But everything a boss has—plush real estate, fawning escorts, cash-fat Swiss bank accounts—has come to him through risk and sacrifice.

Risk scares the soldier. He plays it safe, running safe, low-risk rackets that yield safe, low-risk returns, and because he hedges his bets, his gains on his gambles are nominal. The boss, on the other hand, will bet everything every time. He isn't scared of humiliation or of having to start new. To be boss, you must be ready to bet whatever you most cherish on a long shot. Only then will you win a tenfold reward.

Don't be fooled into thinking that your rise will come easy. You will be obstructed, and you will have to prove yourself to the men who can make you. **Truth: Before you are made, you will be tested.** A day will come when you are called in to do a piece of work; you must agree without hesitation. You must also succeed; failure will block your promotion and you will never father the Family.

Your test will come from the boss. He will need you to kill someone. You will be told to put together a hit squad and carry out the job, and to do it well, leaving no witnesses or evidence trail. You will only get one chance, so do what the boss asks, no matter what it is. If the boss tells you to walk a tightrope a mile high and a thousand feet long, you must walk it, even if, for every ten men who try, nine fall to their death. **Truth: Your destiny waits at the rope.** Your boss, the boss of your boss, and the bosses of past times have crossed the mile-high thousand-foot tightrope; that's why the boss is your boss. Follow suit. Fail, and soldier is as high as you will go. *Boss* is not for the faint of heart.

Truth: There is "only one head of the brotherhood in America," as Joe Masseria said, and your chance at the throne won't come more than once. Even if a shotgun barrel points at your skull, take your chance. Fail, and you will spend the rest of your life in pain. **Truth: "Be it an hour from now or be it tonight or a hundred years from now," as Gotti said, when the chance comes to lead the Family, take it.** Seize every opportunity that leads to the rank of boss.

Truth: If the choices are to be a soldier or die, better to die.

RULE

12

ALIGN WITH HIGH RANK

If he to whom you give your adherence conquers, although he be powerful and you are at his mercy, still he is under obligations to you, and has become your friend; and none are so lost to shame as to destroy with ostentatious ingratitude one who has helped them.

—Niccolò Machiavelli, *The Prince*, 1513

RULE 12:
ALIGN WITH HIGH RANK

It takes many stepping stones, you know, for a man to rise.
None can do it unaided.

—Joe Bonanno

The boss aligns with the influential and the powerful. If you run rum from the maritime limit to the Harlem speaks, you don't court the cop on the beat, you court the commissioner. Control the commissioner and you're safe with the cop on the beat.

Through the powerful you control everyone below them. If a union president can be bought, buy him and the union's locals come with him. If a police commissioner can be bribed, bribe him and you have his captain. Pay off the captain and you have his officers and the streets they patrol. If you need the city, make cozy with the mayor and you have the council and the work force. If you need the state, court the governor's office—even a Trump cannot build a casino without the state's approval.

The same goes within the Family. The boss gives orders to the underboss, who gives orders to the caporegimes, who gives orders to the soldiers; align yourself with the boss. Give him a service he values and an envelope of cash at the turn of the month. When you replace him, you will inherit his underboss, his caporegimes, and his soldiers.

Courting the soldiers is pointless: they have no power. In their company you have nothing to gain and everything to lose. In terms of helping you rise, a soldier is like a gangster working the street without a gun or a construction worker working a building site without a hardhat. Stay away from him, even if he's next of kin. Chop him off as someone did the hands of Bonanno caporegime Sonny Black. Make your underboss and caporegimes seasoned and gray haired. Your friends, your advisers, should be ranking men in the Family, or men outside it on your payroll—a senator, a banker, a newspaper publisher. Your power outside the Family will fortify your power within it.

Your friends should be the police commissioner and the governor. You will need those relationships in times of trial. **Truth: The Family shelters racketeers and gangsters, and a jury will not warm to the testimony of a gangster, even a polished one, for in the eyes of the public a gangster is a parasite.** The commissioner, though, is the law, and the governor is a statesman. They will sway a jury and a weary public, and their support will be good PR when you need it most.

RULE

13

SAY NOTHING

So soon as you impart your design to a discontented man, you supply him with the means of removing his discontent, since by betraying you he can procure for himself every advantage; so that seeing on the one hand certain gain, and on the other a doubtful and dangerous risk, he must either be a rare friend to you, or the mortal enemy of his Prince, if he keep your secret.

—Niccolò Machiavelli, *The Prince*, 1513

RULE 13:
SAY NOTHING
Mum's the word.

Don't ever say anything you don't want played back to you someday.

—John Gotti

If all the fish in the sea kept their mouths shut, they'd never get caught.

—Cosa Nostra saying

If a soldier, be he a friend of mine or a friend of ours, is loose with his tongue, revealing his take in the numbers, giving away the name of his wife and the address of his family, a boss should not interrupt him. Let him talk, but plan to have him killed. He is issuing the order for his own execution.

Truth: Loose talk invites the law and its indictments, decimating the Five Families.

Truth: A talkative soldier will die by the gun, or by the knife, but also by his own words.

The hitman ordered to whack a soldier is unconcerned, since whacking a soldier needs no skill, but moving on a boss demands a steady hand. The boss says little before his men, leading the Family with few words. This discourages plots and conspiracies, as well as infiltration from the outside. **Truth: If a boss is tight with his tongue, his Family will be difficult to breach.**

Where loose talk brings Rudy Giuliani and his agents, silence brings no worries. Where the soldier may ramble, telling stories of hits and spilling the details of the asbestos and concrete rackets, the boss is quiet. He knows that where words are, so are the feds. This is why the boss is a boss and the soldier is a soldier. This is why the boss speaks without speaking; when he orders a hit, he does so by gesture, nodding his head or tapping his chin. He speaks with his eyes, his hands, never with his mouth. It is at the boss's nod, not his verbal order, that soldiers go to war—that mattresses are moved into tenements and lime buries the stench of corpses. To have people killed, speak without speech. Your guilt will be hard to prove.

So when addressing the Family, say only what won't get you indicted. If you need conversation, converse with the maître d' or the gardener.

As boss, you wake up to envious caporegimes and soldiers awaiting your fall. The law and rival factions eavesdrop on your walk-talks and your daughter's pink phone is wiretapped. So is your social club, your chauffeured Jaguar, and your most trusted man. **Truth: Nothing is secret once it has left your mouth.** At dusk, at dawn, and in between, a mole stands before you and behind you. Smoke and mirrors are the face of the Family. Don't be fooled: every smile is a frown in disguise. A boss has no friends—does a friend sit at the table where wealth and power dine? Never trust a man who walks upright and has ten toes, eight fingers, and two thumbs. That man will be careless with what you tell him. Watch your words, and when your trial comes no one can turn state's evidence and bring about your demise.

Truth: Your rackets may be illegal and nineteen corpses may show the marks of your bullets, but those crimes won't ruin you; as sure as the French have a connection, your downfall will come through your tongue. Through what you say, you will unknowingly formulate the plot that puts a bullet in your skull. When the lawman raids the Ravenite, indicting you, your underboss, and your consigliere, the smoking gun will be a recording device carrying your voice. So watch your tongue as you would the secrecy of Cosa Nostra. Long rule will be the result.

The soldier is an open book. He speaks without filters, incriminating himself with every participle. For the boss, mum's the word. Your enemy's ear is nearby. When you thought the walls were deaf, a bug was hidden in the crevices in the floor. The jury will hear the playback in federal court. Your Family and everything you have gained will be no more. You will spend your last hours in Marion Correctional, pleading with your daughter to "send a group picture" of your grandchildren, as John Gotti did. Your properties will be seized, your son will be indicted, and you will die before your daughter has her first toothache.

Black hand

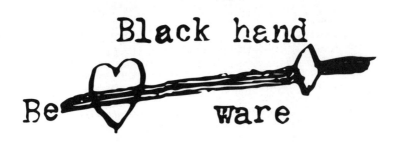

Be ware

what happens

RULE
14

IMPOSE HARSH RULES

Men are either to be kindly treated, or utterly crushed, since they can revenge lighter injuries, but not graver. Wherefore the injury we do to a man should be of a sort to leave no fear of reprisals.

—Niccolò Machiavelli, *The Prince*, 1513

RULE 14:
IMPOSE HARSH RULES

We don't break our captains. We kill them.

—Vincent "Chin" Gigante

The boss calls a meet, summoning his hundred soldiers. There he orders that between sunset and sunrise each man must collect and turn over to him ten troughs of whiskey. Anyone who falls short, he promises, will die, be it a hundred soldiers or one—no exceptions. And be it a hundred soldiers or one, anyone who comes through will keep his life and be given a fifth of Scotch and a night with a good *puttana*.

In the morning, the boss reviews the results. Ninety-nine soldiers have fewer than ten troughs; only one can give him the full number. Without conversation or counsel, the boss must call his underperforming soldiers to the carpet, killing them one by one. After ninety-nine heads have fallen to the floor, the single successful soldier must be awarded said *puttana* and fifth of Scotch. His skill must be recognized, but no more than that, for more will be required of him.

Holding court at the Ravenite, the boss is unable to make contact with his caporegime. He fumes, as John Gotti did to Big Tony Moscatiello, "I called your fucking house five times yesterday! Now, if you're going to disregard my motherfucking phone calls, I'll blow you and that fucking house up! If I ever hear anybody else calls you and you respond within five days, I'll fucking kill you!" Next morning the boss phones his caporegime, to no avail. Five days follow and yet, silence. As promised, the boss must tell his top gunman to put together a team.

By noon the headlines should read: MASSIVE EXPLOSION LEAVES HOME IN RUBBLE—ONE DEAD.

A soldier is hard to manage. He has no freedom and his rackets turn nickels, so if a dollar is to be earned, whether or not it's within the rules, the soldier will go for it. As boss, though, you cannot accept disobedience. You must make clear to your Family that any member found breaking the rules will end up with cement feet. Be it one violator or a hundred, all must feel a bullet penetrating his skull. **Truth: Disobedience is to be dealt with by the gun.**

Didn't Salvatore Maranzano declare that "no man must ever, upon penalty of death, talk about the organization or the Family of which he is a member, not even within his own home"? Didn't Maranzano order that "every man must obey, without question, the orders of the leader above him," and that "no man must ever strike another member, regardless of the provocation"? Didn't he say that "no man can ever covet another's business or another's wife"—and that "if you do, you pay with your life"? Having been clear in your orders, you cannot spare an insubordinate soldier's life. Otherwise your soldiers will see your orders as meaningless and will run amok.

Truth: A soldier learns not from rhetoric but from the bullet. The mere threat of a bullet may not deter him, but the warmth of a bullet will teach him a lot. Or, if he talks too much, cut out his tongue and you'll no longer have to worry about what he says. In dealing with your soldiers, be as direct in your speech as John Gotti: "I'll take your father and I'll put you together in a barrel. Do you want to wake up in the morning and not see your son no more? Is that what you desire? Do you want us to cut your tongue out of your mouth?"

As boss, you will find defiance under every rock. If your response is a threat, you have to mean it. Your Family must know that your word is good. Penalties must be enforced harshly and fast. Shoot everyone who defies you one by one at point-blank range. Cut out the tongue they speak with and the hand they shake with. Stack their limbs in a pile. They will worry you no more.

RULE
15

AVOID ROUTINE

Having always prospered while adhering to one path, he cannot be persuaded that it would be well for him to forsake it. And so when occasion requires the cautious man to act impetuously, he cannot do so and is undone: whereas, had he changed his nature with time and circumstances, his fortune would have been unchanged.

—Niccolò Machiavelli, *The Prince*, 1513

RULE 15:
AVOID ROUTINE

I don't create a pattern in my life. I don't walk my dog 7 o'clock in the morning every morning. I don't go to the same restaurant, sit in the same seat every Tuesday night.

—Michael Franzese

A boss must avoid routine. If you schedule a meet every Friday at the Bergin Hunt, where your soldiers must report on their take, sooner or later your Family will be infiltrated. The law watches you from the east and the Chin from the west. Call your soldiers on a schedule and you will fall.

Say the Family last met on week four, day six, of the first month. The next meet shouldn't match in any way: make it week two, day three, two months later, and your enemies will be scrambled. In everything you do, nothing can be routine. If you often eat with an in-law, change the time of the day, the day of the week, and the restaurant every time. If you sniff a rosebush at noon every Thursday, you will die beside that rosebush.

Truth: A boss is most vulnerable when boxed in by four walls, be it a car, an office, an eatery, or a social club. If routine is a must, do it outside.

Don't commit yourself to any one idea or strategy, for even perfection hides a hairline crack. Fence your estate with twelve-foot walls topped with barbed wire, let barking dogs and armed men loose behind them, sweep the house for bugs and search every crevice—all fine, but meet there routinely and your end will soon come.

RULE
16

KEEP A STASH

I pronounce those able to stand alone to be those who, with the men and money at their disposal, can get together an army fit to take the field against any assailant; and, conversely, I judge those in constant need of help to be those who cannot take the field against their enemies but are obliged to retire behind their walls, and to defend themselves there.

—Niccolò Machiavelli, *The Prince*, 1513

RULE 16:
KEEP A STASH
Money speaks every language.

I got plenty of dough.

—Charlie "Lucky" Luciano

Truth: Dollars buy answers to everything. The boss should keep a large account in a Zurich bank, held for the morning when his home is raided by the feds. **Truth: The amount of your stash should be five times your monthly take.** If your racket turns $1 million a month, you should have $5 million put away. **Truth: The Lincoln rides as smooth as butter and the signet ring shines, but more than diamonds and gold, the luxury automobiles and residences, a boss must have money.** At your darkest hour—the day when you're least prepared, when the sirens blare and the Family rebels—your Zurich accounts will buy you time.

When the state indicts you, your legal bill will be $700,000 and your bail will be $350,000. When your rival kidnaps your next of kin, the ransom note will include six zeros. And when the IRS raids your offices, humiliating you publicly and handing you a tax bill, your rackets will bottom out, reducing your revenue. **Truth: If your cup is dry, you are useful to none.** You must be able to pay your creditors and partners, and your stash must be big enough to protect you.

A boss should not seem to be penniless. He should appear and be cash rich. The public should see him as wealthy. **Truth: The poor man brings shame on himself and his kinfolk despise him.** If he doesn't have enough to buy or trade with, he is a "crumb, working and slaving for a few bucks," in Lucky Luciano's eyes. He must resort to the dirtiest kinds of labor, like cleaning toilets. He works until his hands are callused. Meanwhile the boss's coffers overflow with cash, valuables, things that glitter and shine.

So when you become boss, follow suit. Pile your dollars beyond count. Every mattress, shoebox, car trunk, duffel bag, and hole in the wall should be crammed with cash. As sure as Tommy Lucchese had no right forefinger and thumb, a day will come when you will have to come up with payola. You will need to draw on your stash and pay where payment is due.

Bribery and corruption are confidants of the boss and eat envelopes of dollars. Every deed has a price, every favor hides a motive, nothing is done for love. So save your emotions for your family and apply logic and brute force to filling your cash coffer so high that it can never be spent.

RULE

17

LOYALTY IS A LIE

Of men it may generally be affirmed that they are thankless, fickle, false, studious to avoid danger, greedy of gain, devoted to you while you are able to confer benefits upon them, and ready, as I said before, while danger is distant, to shed their blood, and sacrifice their property, their lives, and their children for you; but in the hour of need they turn against you.

—Niccolò Machiavelli, *The Prince*, 1513

RULE 17:
LOYALTY IS A LIE
Show none, expect none.

When I looked around the neighborhood, I found out that the kids wasn't the only crooks. We was surrounded by crooks, and plenty of them was guys who were supposed to be legit, like the landlords and storekeepers and the politicians and cops on the beat. All of them was stealing from somebody.

—Charlie "Lucky" Luciano

A soldier is easily suborned. His price is cheap: he will barter his loyalty for a small share in a racket and offer you false friendship. **Truth: If the opportunity arises, a soldier will kill his boss in a jiffy.**

The soldier's king is the dollar. He will sell his loyalty for a buck. Be he outsider, boss, underboss, caporegime, or soldier, what man's honor is not available for a price? **Truth: If humans have walked the planet for a millennium, then for a millennium they have sold their honor cheap.**

If there is a likeness between a soldier and a boss, it is their lack of respect for loyalty. They may charge different prices, but neither the soldier nor the boss exists who will not betray his partners. The difference is that where betrayal worries a soldier, it gratifies a boss, who sees it as the price of leadership.

As boss, you can't expect to hold all the wealth, all the power, without your soldiers betraying you. Betrayal is to be expected for a boss. If it hasn't happened yet, you are a weak leader, owning nothing valuable enough for others to want. A soldier's rank being low, it is relatively free of envy, but a boss should be ready for the stool pigeons to sing. **Truth: Those who once protected you are those you will eventually need to be protected from.** And if you find yourself staring into the barrel of a revolver, the man with his finger on the trigger was once your best friend.

Once you are boss, and the Family is under your control, watch every eye. You are respected by rich and poor, your name opens doors in high government offices, but your soldiers curse you when you can't hear them: "All he's interested in is making money." And your underboss: "He's a stupid pig." So trust no one. Everyone who bows to kiss your signet also resents you.

The one man you can trust is your enemy: if he promises to kill you, he will do his best to make that promise good. Contempt moves a man better than affection. If you ever find yourself on a hitman's kill list, you can trust him to try. But you can't trust anyone else.

A soldier trusts. That's why he works for you. Only the weak take orders. The boss considers himself superior to almost everyone, so he doesn't ask for permission, he grants it. **Truth: To the extent that a soldier embraces ideals of loyalty, that is his weakness.** Don't follow him into the grave; let him die. He lives a sad life, wondering why he is so often betrayed, worrying about getting shot, not realizing that what's killing him is his foolish trust. As sure as the sun rises in the morning, people lack honor. A great many great men were knifed in the back and died at the hands of a trusted confidant, a made man in the same Cosa Nostra.

You don't have to look far to find an enemy, nor will he be well hidden. Look to your right: who's there? **Truth: When the time is ripe, it will be your top loyalist—your right hand—who riddles you with bullets and leaves you face down in your own blood.** As the vultures eat your carcass, that loyalist will sleep with your spouse.

RULE

18

PAY YOUR
SOLDIERS WELL

To keep his Minister good, the Prince should be considerate of him, dignifying him, enriching him, binding him to himself by benefits, and sharing with him the honours as well as the burthens of the State, so that the abundant honours and wealth bestowed upon him may divert him from seeking them at other hands.

—Niccolò Machiavelli, *The Prince*, 1513

RULE 18:
PAY YOUR SOLDIERS WELL

It's remarkable how loyal people will be when you look after them as well as we did. We gave them incentives and rewards for good work. When they came up with useful proposals, we praised them and lined their pockets.

—Meyer Lansky

When money is scarce and the rackets are turning losses, the noble become thieves, the priests become pimps, and the fierce become cowards. **Truth: The most honorable soldier will ditch his loyalty if he's not paid.** Who labors in the muck without a reason to? **Truth: A soldier only works the junk and numbers rackets because they yield a take.** He runs speaks full of drunkards in the expectation of being a good earner. If you ever look at your soldier and see his jacket dark with bloodstains and his trousers holed at the knee, take note that he had a hard day and should be paid for his work.

As boss, you must pay your soldiers their due. In return, they will work their rackets well and grant you loyalty. And you must pay your soldiers better than your rivals would, for if they can be easily bought, your Family will fall. **Truth: It is better to kill a man than to abuse a man.** Abuse your soldier and in one way or another his pain will come back to you.

As much as pay, be it high or low, a man needs respect. Paying him $2 for a job worth $4 will give him pause—he will sell your secrets and bring the law to your door. To pay a man his due is a show of respect. As boss, don't cheapen your soldier's honor by underpaying him. Pay him well and, as New York State Supreme Court Justice Thomas Aurelio told Luciano Family boss Frank Costello, he will "want to assure you" of his loyalty and to prove that "it is unwavering."

To prevent your Family from falling into a war, give your soldiers three times what the market will bear. Give them the finest Scotch, aged vino, the freshest mozzarella and tomato, linguine with pesto, a flaky cannoli, and newly brewed latte. **Truth: If the boss is fat, the soldiers must be fat too.**

A soldier's loyalty can be bought cheap. On money, meet what he asks—it won't put a dent in the Family holdings. **Truth: Pay a soldier his due, which will be nominal, and he will work his rackets with diligence, seeking neither to be promoted nor to leave.**

RULE

19

SPEAK THE LANGUAGE OF THE SOLDIER

States which, upon their acquisition, are joined on to the ancient dominions of the Prince who acquires them, are either of the same race and tongue as the people of these dominions, or they are not. When they are, there is great ease in retaining them…. But when States are acquired in a country differing in language, usages, and laws, difficulties multiply, and great good fortune as well as address are needed to overcome them.

—Niccolò Machiavelli, *The Prince*, 1513

RULE 19:
SPEAK THE LANGUAGE OF THE SOLDIER

Maranzano could make everyone in a crowded room think he was talking to him individually. He tailored his speeches to the mentality of his audience. To a simple audience, he spoke in parables; to a more intelligent audience, he proclaimed ideas.

—Joe Bonanno

As boss, speak to the Family in a language they know.

Suppose, like Tony "Ducks" Corallo, you have told your crew, "Anybody fucking around with junk"—selling narcotics—"they got to be killed." But you discover that half your soldiers, and half your rivals, are "fucking around with junk." What to do? **Truth: Half your Family and half your rivals aren't wrong.** The soldier is a hood, a gangster. In the streets, he goes for the money and lives by the law of hard knocks. You can dress him in tailored suits and chauffeur him in a Lincoln, but don't think he's white collar. If you made him as a gangster, then a gangster he is. So don't stymie his initiative. Leave him to his work. Turn a blind eye. And when you speak, speak as a gangster. Otherwise your words will fall on deaf ears.

Truth: If you live among fools, then speak foolish, walk foolish, and act foolish. When you swing the pendulum toward sense, do it slowly and carefully. If you're trying to legitimize the Family, moving it into white rackets, make soldiers with white-collar histories. Make a blue-collar soldier work white-collar rackets and uprising will follow. **Truth: A kennel provides food and shelter, but an abandoned dog won't go in, for what's unknown is unnerving.** So work a soldier in the rackets in which he is skilled, and when you talk to him, speak the language of his work rather than yours. When your soldiers meet with you, speak in language they understand. Speak to a soldier in the language of a banker and what he'll hear is "Blah blah blah."

A soldier would rather hate what he understands than love what he does not. Speak to his way of thinking. Narcotics are in demand; let your soldier work them. To ban what is in demand will corrode your Family. **Truth: The soldier deals in narcotics because the profits are immense.** Are dollars from junk less green than dollars from extortion? Don't run a Family made up of illegit rackets and yet order your soldiers to be legit. Speak what seems to them a foreign language and you'll end up with a bullet in your head.

A soldier doesn't think with the psyche of a boss. Where a boss must have foresight, a soldier is myopic, seeing only what's right there. So don't say anything to a soldier that he can't understand. **Truth: The soldier has the vision of the blind and the hearing of the deaf.** If he could see and hear as a boss, you would be dead, because he would have killed you and taken your place. As boss, you must see up the mountain and beyond to the other side of it, where the soldier's vision cannot go, but don't talk to him about what you find there. Instead, guide him to and up the mountain. When you reach the top, he will see what you see, and will follow you farther. But tell him what you see before then and he will mark you down as crazy—and your soldiers will end up killing you, afraid that you will bring the Family down.

RULE

20

TAKE IT TO THE MATTRESS

Enemies who remain, although vanquished, in their own homes, have power to hurt.

—Niccolò Machiavelli, *The Prince*, 1513

RULE 20:
TAKE IT TO THE MATTRESS
When it's time to kill, kill everyone.

If a man is in a fight, then he must fight to the end.

—Joe Bonanno

If a new direction must be sought, half the Family will be with you, half will be against you, and neither side will benefit you. If half are against you, more will join them; and of those who are with you, one will be Donnie Brasco. So you can't trust the entire lot.

The new direction will come through war. The leaders of the previous regime must die, along with their supporters. **Truth: When a boss dies, his faithful must go with him.** Drop the hammer: kill the sons, and the sons of the sons if they are in *the life*. If anyone is spared, make it wives and daughters, for women are not part of *this thing of ours*. Burn everything to ash. Leave nothing standing. Half of the caporegimes must die, since their allegiance is with their boss, whom you have killed. To lead the Family in a new direction, you must appoint a new administration, for as long as the old-timers remain, you are not safe.

Start a war and the Commission will oppose you. Cosa Nostra is a secret society; its strength lies in privacy and calm. Wage war and you turn the bosses against you. The Commission comprises seven Families, the five in New York and two more. How can your single Family resist the other six? A boss, then, will avoid war at all costs. Going to the mattresses is the last resort—but if it becomes necessary, the war should be swift, killing as many as possible in the shortest time. Tommy guns should spray bullets, leaving carcasses in the street and blood in the gutters. The air should reek of death.

Why pussyfoot in war? **Truth: When war comes, a boss should think like John Gotti and "kill all the cocksuckers in the whole Family."** To waver in combat is to bring about your demise. Better for the newspapers to write about a bloody day once than to write about a bloody day ten days in a row. If on Valentine's Day you have seven enemies, pile seven bodies before sunrise and the headlines will read "Saint Valentine's Day Massacre" in the morning but not on the day after. Kill a man a day for seven consecutive days, though, and the press and the police will declare you a public enemy and the Commission will retire you.

As boss, put down every man who opposes you. Be brutal; your enemies don't deserve a merciful killing. Shoot them, slash their throats, steal their money, and take over their rackets. Show your strength. Put fear in your enemies' minds. They will say, "He's nuts! This guy will take your father and he'll put you together in a barrel!" (As Gotti said when advising his daughter to use his reputation to protect her son from bullying.) Don't worry about the blood you've spilled, for your rivals would have done the same to you, had they been able—they would have taken your rackets and made your children orphans.

RULE
21

BE HONORABLE

They who become Princes...by virtuous paths, acquire their Princedoms with difficulty, but keep them with ease.

—Niccolò Machiavelli, *The Prince*, 1513

RULE 21:
BE HONORABLE
Your word is your bond.

I did forty years in the street with the worst fucking people, and on a handshake, we always kept our word.

—Anthony "Gaspipe" Casso

If you work petty rackets on the streets, you interact with bosses of various levels. If you are an associate, your boss is a soldier; if a soldier, your boss is a caporegime; if a caporegime, your boss is an underboss; if an underboss, your boss is the boss.

Whatever your level, be honorable and efficient in dealing with your boss. Your work may require you to be cunning and cutthroat, but in the eyes of the boss, be a man of honor. If you are a pickpocket, don't be seen as such: as you slip your hand into a man's pocket, removing his wallet and watch, do it with a smile. Your reality doesn't matter; be a pimp or a thief, but smile as you work and people will like you. **Truth: The truth of a man yields meager dividends. You will always get more out of a good facade.**

Suppose your boss tells you to fetch a coffee and a cannoli, and then within twenty minutes two more. Don't argue—instead, scamper off and come back with the flakiest Italian pastry you can find and a hot cup of java made from freshly ground and brewed beans. And do it fast.

No man becomes boss without making alliances during his formative years. To be a boss, you must first please a boss: you must be a good earner and make whatever payments you have shaken hands on. And for the health of your rackets, people must know your word is good. The Commission will OK the ouster even of a boss if his word is shaky. As you lead your soldiers and administration, whatever you tell them they should trust. A promise made should be a promise honored, even if it means leaving the bedside of a dying spouse.

A soldier cannot rise in rank without a boss's approval. If he is to become a skipper, the boss must give the order. **Truth: The man who will grant you authority is a man already holding authority.** And since men rise in rank according to the degree to which they are trusted, keep your word. Promise the boss ten laughs within a minute and you must deliver; if the tenth laugh comes on second sixty-one, your honor is in question. You will stay a soldier.

RULE
22

TAKE YOUR BULLET

Never suffer your designs to be crossed in order to avoid war, since war is not so to be avoided, but is only deferred to your disadvantage.

—Niccolò Machiavelli, *The Prince*, 1513

RULE 22:
TAKE YOUR BULLET
Pain is to be embraced.

How many of these guys come tell me, "I feel sorry you got trouble." I don't.
I don't need that. I ain't got no trouble. I'm going to be all right.

—John Gotti

Everywhere a boss goes, be it the whiskey distillery or the Waldorf barber-shop, he must embrace the pain that comes with leadership. Lucky Luciano had a scarred cheek and a lazy eye, both left by a knifing; should you be similarly scarred, consider yourself Lucky. Every boss has taken a beating before he was in a position to authorize one. **Truth: If your body is unmarked by bullet holes, you walk without limping, and you have all your fingers and thumbs, but you are nevertheless named boss, your rank is a hoax.** The bosses are manipulating you, and either your death is near or you're about to be indicted. You thought that you had power but you will quickly discover that you are Fat Tony Salerno carrying the bags for Vincent "Chin" Gigante.

To be a Cosa Nostra boss, you must first feel the pain of war. As Joe Bonanno wrote in his autobiography, you must ride with "one pistol, three machine guns, and 600 rounds of ammunition." You must avoid your home and office, letting no one but those closest to you know where you are from one day to the next. You must be ready not to see your wife for months. Your priority is winning the war. You will see your wife when the war has ended. Every bullet wound and broken limb will prime you for Boss. To order soldiers to sleep on a mattress and be obeyed, you must yourself know what it is to be wounded and clutching a pistol.

Just as Cosa Nostra brings life, Cosa Nostra brings death. As a soldier and at every rank thereafter, you will know hard times. Bullets will graze your hat and pierce your flesh, you will feel the knife at your throat, and you will spend long nights on the mattresses, taking shut-eye with a gun in your hand. It's those times that qualify you as godfather. Even then, tough times will continue. The law will knock, indictments will come: embrace them. Welcome the man who plots against you, and do it happily. That way you'll be seasoned, primed for whatever will come, and your rivals will fall faster than they rise.

A boss does not worry. He relishes the pain that makes a soldier suffer. While the boss is oiling his tommy guns, the soldier is cowering: gunfire sickens his stomach and buckles his knees. That's why the soldier is a soldier and the boss is a boss. The sound of a gun is what you have to go through before advancing to Boss—so, enjoy it.

When the time comes for you to ask the Commission to approve you to lead your Family, what will you have left to worry about? Like Gotti, you already "got nothing but heartache." You have stood in the crosshairs of would-be assassins, you have felt the blows of cops' billy clubs, you have waited in shackles before magistrates, you have taken your bullet. The pains of tomorrow don't worry you. You head *this thing of ours*. You decide who lives and who dies.

RULE

23

KEEP YOUR
HANDS CLEAN

*Princes should devolve on others those matters that entail responsibility,
and reserve to themselves those that relate to grace and favour.*

—Niccolò Machiavelli, *The Prince*, 1513

RULE 23:
KEEP YOUR HANDS CLEAN
Dirty work is for the underboss.

I got to be careful of my associates. They'll accuse me of consorting with questionable characters.

—Frank Costello

Men of honor are dashing, formal, and sophisticated. They meet with muck reluctantly: you will not find a boss in a dirty alley. Consort with dirt and you yourself will get dirty.

As boss, keep dirt at arm's length. Steer clear of pimps and pushers and don't carry a gun. Relax among your own people, men of your tradition, for if your fellow bosses stumble on you fraternizing with the lowly, you will be judged and your opportunities will shrink. Respect the rank to which you have risen and be vigilant about your involvements. Otherwise politicians will turn down your bribes, no matter how high. **Truth: If your hands are seen to be soiled, handling money from whores and junk, people who think themselves honorable, or want to appear as such, will turn away.**

Suppose your Family is full of insubordinate soldiers. Your underboss suggests that the most troublesome be killed. Approve those killings, but needless to say, don't do them yourself. A boss should only raise a hand in defense of his own life. Everything else is to be done by a soldier on orders from the underboss. No boss should mingle with street hoodlums and bums, for he has graduated to the topmost rank. **Truth: Bosses talk to bosses.** If a boss must speak, he should speak only to the Commission and his administration. The one to communicate his orders to his caporegimes and soldiers is the underboss.

As boss, leave behind the circles you have risen from. In your green days you worked the streets, acting on orders from above. Now that you're at the top, never do that again. Bask in your rank. Take tête-à-têtes with other bosses and the city elites, people with apparently clean hands. If you sense a problem in the Family, have your underboss clean it up. The father may want a piece of work done, but setting it up is the job of the underboss.

The soldier works in the muck; the boss drinks wine and plays the horses. But every boss has his day of reckoning, and when it comes, it comes brutally: he dies in a hail of gunfire or is sentenced to life in Marion. So while you have the reins, relish them. Take your shut-eye in the Waldorf Astoria or the Majestic. Enjoy the nightlife of the Beverly Club, dine in L'Aiglon and the Norse Grill, and lie with Virginia Hill— "the best goddamned cocksucker in the world," by her own account— for you are the boss.

RULE

24

EVERY MAN HAS A PRICE

Men, thinking to better their condition, are always ready to change masters.

—Niccolò Machiavelli, *The Prince*, 1513

RULE 24:
EVERY MAN HAS A PRICE
Find it and pay it.

It doesn't matter whether it is a banker, a businessman, or a gangster, his pocketbook is always attractive.

—New York Mayor William O'Dwyer

In matters of the dollar, no one is clean. Everyone is innately self-interested and the dollar brings that out. If you hear someone claiming to be a man of honor, watch your wallet.

If you want to test a man's honor, give him an envelope full of cash. Before you take your next breath, he will morph before your eyes. A man trying to climb in the Family will seize every opportunity that will fatten the envelope. Has there been a day in history when no one has sold their honor cheap? As boss, use payola liberally, for the dollar is a truer measure than title, rank, or family.

Truth: Before a man brews his morning beans, before he washes his body in the suds of the shower, before he puts on his trousers and ties a Windsor around his neck, he stands as naked as you do. Dressed, he is no more than a hog in a suit, and will eat his children if eating them will profit him. Don't be fooled by his charm, don't be flattered by his sophisticated vocabulary or his knowledge of wine; he is available for pennies. Be he senator, judge, or governor, he can be bought. If the senator plays the races, find him a horse; if the judge is a womanizer, send him Virginia Hill; if the governor is campaigning, buy him delegates. Poke and pry until you find his price. Then pay him fivefold. Lucky Luciano claimed to be "buying influence all over Manhattan, from lower Broadway all the way up to Harlem, and even across the Hudson beyond the Palisades in Jersey." Do the same.

Truth: Honor is a hoax; the real art is self-preservation. This is why a day will come when Cosa Nostra will implode: its members will serve themselves over the interest of the organization.

As boss, use men's greed. Pay someone distinguished to be your character witness, testifying to your integrity and respectability. You will need the legislators and the judges, the bellhops and the maître d's—grease them. A cache of cash will bend the most righteous knee. A man will die for whatever he most wants; find his price, pay it, and your demands will be met.

As far back as the *Mano Nera* gangs, soldiers have been motivated by greed, but in that they are no different from anyone. What will the judge or congressman do for money? Are either the writers or the enforcers of the law immune from corruption? **Truth: The statesman and the magistrate are "no-good selfish cocksuckers,"** as Lucky Luciano said of his longtime partner Joe Adonis. A boss knows that all men can be bought. If you're facing life in prison, think like John Gotti: "We'll put together four to five million, bribe a president, and get a pardon like Hoffa did." **Truth: Give a man a full half of a big score, it won't be enough.** The next day he'll want more. Poor or rich, he wears a tag showing his price. The numbers are different, but you should pay them both.

A soldier's price is cheap. So buy him cheap, exploit him, and then shoot him. Don't be so foolish as to spare his life or he will revenge himself later. **Truth: Rob a man, sleep with his wife, malign him behind his back—all can be forgiven.** But if he finds you have exploited and deceived him he will hate you until his clock ticks no more.

Only a boss cannot be bought, for his price is nonmonetary. Your dollars are devalued with a boss since he already has wealth. All you can offer him is trade in the form of service. So no matter what the trade is, don't imagine you own a boss. At best you are his partner. He owns you as much as you own him.

RULE

25

TAKE WHAT'S YOURS

There are two ways of contending, one in accordance with the laws, the other by force; the first of which is proper to men, the second to beasts. But since the first method is often ineffectual, it becomes necessary to resort to the second.

—Niccolò Machiavelli, *The Prince*, 1513

RULE 25:
TAKE WHAT'S YOURS
Greatness is seized, not given.

I wanted it, so I took it.

—Charlie "Lucky" Luciano

By examining a boss's journey we can learn from his genius. The bosses of tomorrow will model their ambitions on the bosses of today; the bosses of today have modeled their ambitions on the bosses of yesterday. The hero of today's boss might be, say, Don Salvatore Maranzano, a boss of yesterday. Today's boss may mock Maranzano's ways of doing things, but he still hopes that he will one day be as great.

To be a boss, copy a boss. **Truth: The boss you copy got everything he has by theft.** Like Frank Costello, "Everything he knows, he stole." Wealth, influence, respectability—all stolen. A boss doesn't ask, he takes. If wealth and influence are what you're looking for, you will have to steal them, for nothing valuable is free.

Everything that glitters and gleams, everything that buys: the boss has it. He has valuables and piles of dollars a million high, constantly restocked from envelopes stuffed with his take. Meanwhile the soldier works endlessly, rising early and going home late. He drives a jalopy while the boss is driven in a Lincoln. The boss takes a piece of every dollar the soldier earns. And though the soldier's profit comes at a painful cost—bullet shards and stab wounds—at the end of the week he has crumbs while the boss is fat.

Truth: The boss eats from two plates, his own and his soldiers'. The soldier is the low man on the totem pole, yet it is his work that generates the Family's wealth. Loansharking and numbers, both of them soldier rackets, bring in big cash. **Truth: The boss swindles the soldier.** A crook and a trickster, he earns off the soldier's labor. For every ten cases of whiskey that the Family cuts, the boss drinks nine. "Everything you get goes into my pot," "Joe the Boss" Masseria told Lucky Luciano, and "if you don't like it, that's too fucking bad." The whiskey belonged to Joe the Boss. If Joe wanted to, he would take Lucky's whiskey and "drink it all himself."

There is no honorable pathway to *Boss*. Look beyond a boss's rationalizations and you'll see he has double-crossed his way up. On his rise, he has killed every gent, gal, and youngster in his way. Crime Families and domestic families were decimated, friends were made rivals, partners were cheated out of their end. So if you hear of a stash in your partner's hideaway, lift it in the wee hours and spend it as if it belonged to you. Given the chance, that's what your partner would do to you—if he treats you to lunch and a day at the track, you may be funding your own excursion without knowing it.

Truth: In your green days, your efforts will go unrewarded. Open up a new racket, gross millions for the Family, enable your boss to buy real estate—your take will go unchanged. If you want wealth and recognition, you will have to take it. It will not be given to you. Rules will have to be broken, trust will have to be shattered, a boss will have to be killed.

RULE
26

HONOR THE BOSS

Let it be seen that you take no offense in hearing the truth.

—Niccolò Machiavelli, *The Prince*, 1513

RULE 26:
HONOR THE BOSS
When you shoot him, shoot him in the face.

[Tom] Reina had to get it face-to-face, according to the rules. Vito told me that when Reina saw him, he started to smile and wave his hand. When he done that, Vito blew his head off.

—Charlie "Lucky" Luciano

Truth: To rise in the Family, every boss has had to learn what it is to feel the breeze of a bullet zipping past his ear or to hobble off wounded, barely escaping an assassin. To become boss, you must put your life on the line. Your boss, like you, has peddled nickel deals with bloody hands. He too has spent time on the mattresses, not knowing whether his last hour had come. The very boss whom you're now vying to oust ran petty rackets and carried out the orders of the administration. So if you want to lead the Family, don't shame him behind his back. Treat him with honor and respect, knowing that to reach the rank he holds, he fought just as you fight. He did not become boss by chance. So kneel to your boss, pucker your lips, and press them against his pinky signet ring.

To be a boss, conduct yourself as a boss. Don't rob him of his ceremonial ousting. The soldier is weak; he whispers in the meet, disrespecting the boss, picking holes in the boss's plans. And if he plots an execution, it will be a cowardly one: to be shot dead, the boss must lower his head or turn his back. **Truth: The soldier is a coward, for only a coward shoots a man in the back.** If a boss is shot dead in his sleep, suspect a soldier.

Your boss has guided and mentored you, given you direction and reward. He does not deserve to die with his eyes closed. For everything he has given the Family, he does deserve a painless death. A soldier—a cutthroat, a thief, a perjurer—might shoot a boss in the body, risking injury and damage rather than mortality. He is not to be admired. Give a boss his due: let him stare down the barrel of a sawed-off, then split his head in two.

When you were a soldier, the boss worked you. He called you away from your child's baptism; he got fat off your labor. So he deserves his bullet—but he also deserves a dignified end. When you move on your boss, invite him for lunch at the Nuova Villa Tammaro in Coney Island. Feast him, laugh at his jokes, play klob with him, honor his cheek and signet with a final kiss, then excuse yourself from the table and come back with your team, guns blazing at his head. Leave him face down in his spaghetti. Don't mangle his body or inflict pain; a boss deserves respect. Look him in the eyes, then treat him to a coup de grâce. This will not be an open-casket funeral.

Now that your boss is a corpse, the Family is under your oxter. **Truth: You too may die face down in a plate of spaghetti, and you should welcome that fate.**

RULE

27

THE END JUSTIFIES
THE MEANS

To slaughter fellow-citizens, to betray friends, to be devoid of honour, pity, and religion, cannot be counted as merits, [but] these are means which may lead to power.

—Niccolò Machiavelli, *The Prince*, 1513

RULE 27:
THE END JUSTIFIES THE MEANS

[Tom] Reina was a man of his word, he had culture, and he was a very honorable Italian.... But he had to be eliminated so I could keep on living and keep on moving up.

—Charlie "Lucky" Luciano

No matter what troubles come today, the boss knows that tomorrow will bring rewards, for he plans every step to lead to a set destination. He may even take two strategic steps backward, plotting them to advance him four steps forward. **Truth: Don't bet against a boss who seems to be slipping, for victory comes not at the race's midpoint but at its flag.** Triumph comes at dusk; don't stumble over the worries of dawn.

History will not question the way a boss has risen, since he will be remembered not for the trail of broken souls that lines his yesterdays but for the works that survive his tomorrows. So, on your journey toward leading the Family, let no one slow your progress. Suppose an honorable man, your topmost loyalist and advocate, stands in your way: kill him. Sink his feet in cement and stick to your path. The end justifies the means.

Truth: On your rise, innocents must perish. You will have to kill the honorable. Outsiders undeserving of death will be made corpses and fed to the fishes. Should the boss tell you to kill your spouse's brother, you will oblige, or else stay a soldier forever. You will shoot him in the back of the head, chop him up, and put his limbs where they'll never be found. **Truth: As Colombo Family underboss Sonny Franzese said, "It's better to take that half-an-hour, an hour, to get rid of the body than it is to leave the body on the street."**

Truth: In Cosa Nostra, no one rises in rank without sin.

And you can't let anything stop you from rising in rank. Death is better than failure. **Truth: When you become boss, the way you got there will be annulled.** Martin Gosch and Leonard Katz will write books on you and the public will lap them up. Don't think about the men who have died on your watch, for your great works will outlive your heartbeat.

If you have risen to *Boss*, toasted with Frank Sinatra, and grown rich, who will care how many men you killed and how many lives you ruined? History will remember you for your accomplishments, not for the men who died along the way. The public will fawn over you, scholars will study your moves, and your portrait will hang with the greats. What you wanted to be, you became. You are the boss.

RULE

28

BUILD RELATIONSHIPS

The road to Princedom lies either through the favour of the people or of the nobles.

—Niccolò Machiavelli, *The Prince*, 1513

RULE 28:
BUILD RELATIONSHIPS

Well-charactered people you don't need introductions to; you just meet automatically.

—Willie Moretti

A boss cannot lead his Family without backing from the Commission, connected men who underpin his power. No matter his strength, without connections even the capo di tutti capi will fall.

At every rank—soldier or caporegime, underboss or boss—you must maintain relationships. In everything you do, court favor. If your caporegime is to marry, send a full envelope—he will be indebted to you and your administration and will respect you. If a favored soldier works the slots, authorize stickers for his machines telling other families and bribed police officers that they are mob run and not to be touched—he too will feel indebted and will owe you loyalty. Both men of honor and outsiders should respect you and what you do. Take every opportunity to strengthen your relationships both in and outside the Family; make those relationships good and your fellow bosses will send their soldiers to the mattresses on your behalf.

Truth: As sure as a boss pricks the finger of the newly inducted, your authority will be challenged. As boss, you will face endless scrutiny from up-and-comers hungry for power. To protect yourself, build alliances with your peers. Association with the well-heeled and the respected will insulate you from your rivals. When

infighting and disloyalty arise, you will be equipped to line your
enemies up and lay them down.

Popularity with reporters will get you favorable coverage in the press;
popularity with the judiciary will get your indictments dismissed. Even
the most senior boss, the capo di tutti capi, cannot lead his Family without friends. Be liked by both low and high society and you will rule
without interference. You will snip roses and live into your gray days,
dying free and of natural causes.

RULE

29

RESPECT YOUR PUBLIC

It is essential for a Prince to be on a friendly footing with his people,
since, otherwise, he will have no resource in adversity.

—Niccolò Machiavelli, *The Prince*, 1513

RULE 29:
RESPECT YOUR PUBLIC

I got a million people who... would cry just to be able to be here to see me.

—John Gotti

As a lowly soldier you worked relatively unwatched. Neither rats nor detectives looked over your shoulder too much, and in kicking your profits up to the bosses, you kept only the smaller part for yourself. As your rackets matured, though, so did your profits. You rose from Brooklyn hoodlum to a dapper man wearing a peacoat and driving a Mercedes.

Now, as boss, you lead a vast enterprise and your name appears in the headlines. As leader of your Family, you are a target. For you as for Frank Costello, every nook holds "a lot of guys trying to get ahead by climbing on your back." **Truth: Vultures get fat by eating the fattened, and what better to eat than a man with pockets full of cash?** Try as you may to avoid it, as boss you will face the scrutiny that comes with leadership. But if you win the respect of the public, you will cut your burdens in half.

You may be rich and your rackets may be white collar, but alienate the public, make them want you lynched, and your feet will surely dangle. So seize every opportunity to win the public over. On turkey day, give out stuffed birds; on Christmas, give children scooters; when it's hot, open the hydrants to treat the young to a soak. As boss, tend to your public assiduously. Build playgrounds and host fireworks parades.

A boss will price-gouge his public, charging the poor an extra dollar for a loaf. He will extort the moms and pops and if caught he will pay off the magistrate. The boss's interest is the Family, not the public. If he hands out turkeys and goody bags, he does it to deceive the public—his real concern is his pocketbook.

To the boss, if the public is fooled and suffers losses, that is its own fault. Outsiders are "a bunch of crumbs asking to be taken," Lucky Luciano said. The muck beneath your feet is not your problem; you serve the Family, your family, and nothing else. But big oil pays handsomely for public relations even as it ruins the planet the public inhabits, and as boss, you should do the same. Make the public love you and when the law hauls you before the judge, the jury will be swayed by the mob out front calling for your acquittal.

When you walk down the street, tip your hat to the guys, kiss the hands of the girls, and drop a twenty in the cup of the beggars. Make the community in which you grew up sing your name. If one mouth goes unfed, you have failed in your communal duties. You are rich; spend some of your money on courting the public's favor. If your community wants to see a movie, "give them a movie theater," as Luciano did. Luciano was setting up extortion rackets when he was ten; he pimped, bootlegged, killed, bribed, waged war, sold narcotics, organized the Commission. And yet, after he died, in exile in Italy in 1962, a local said, "It's incredible how much good this man did."

RULE

30

START EARLY

Because the mere fact of a private person rising to be a Prince presupposes either merit or good fortune, it will be seen that the presence of one or other of these two conditions lessens, to some extent, many difficulties. And yet, he who is less beholden to Fortune has often in the end the better success.

—Niccolò Machiavelli, *The Prince*, 1513

RULE 30:
START EARLY
Be boss in everything you do.

From the time I got to Italy [after World War II], I went heavy into the black market. Pretty soon, I had a fleet of old fishing boats coming and going. If you think we made big profits from bootlegging in the States in the twenties, it didn't compare to the Italian black market. In less than six months, I almost doubled my bankroll.

—Charlie "Lucky" Luciano

Truth: Bosses win. Exiled, deported, stripped of rackets and cash, as Lucky Luciano was—nothing breaks a boss. Wherever your loafers touch down, be the boss.

The soldier is a bum. He has moments of achievement but his name is mud and his life is beyond his control. A boss, on the other hand: wherever he stands, he leads. Whether in the Great Meadow prison in upstate New York or the Sicilian village of Lercara Friddi, all are humbled by the presence of the boss. If you are enduring the hospitality of the state, the warden should cater to your every demand, your fellow inmates should seek your advice and beg your favor, and the guards should let you come and go as you wish. If exiled in Italy, you should take control of the black market and double your bankroll, as Luciano did. Your name should ring the town's bells and draw chants from its people. Every soldier should offer you his trigger finger without cost.

Truth: If the boss is a boss, he is the boss every time the clock strikes twelve and at every hour between. He is a boss by day and a boss by night. He is a boss in wealth and in poverty. If you've reached *Boss*, then you're the boss all the time, whether the time is heaven or hell. You're sentenced to fifty years in Dannemora? Don't break. Lead your Family from prison, relaying your orders through Frank Costello and Meyer Lansky.

Those who reach *Boss* have always genetically been bosses. When they were soldiers they made top dollar. If they were hit men they were the deadliest in the Family. As caporegimes they ran the premium rackets. A boss is easily recognized, for he is a leader of men. His kingship is apparent by the line of "well-charactered people" (in Willie Moretti's phrase) who come to him for counsel at the barbershop in the Waldorf Astoria. **Truth: If you are a boss, your advice will be sought.** The fathers of the other Families will relish your smarts, respecting your every request.

But squander your green years on nickel rackets and then try to about-face and become boss when you're going gray, and failure will find you. Time has yet to record a man who waited till late to become boss. **Truth: Once your path is set, it can't be reversed.** If you were a drunkard and a womanizer coming up, sniffing coke through a dollar bill, napping till noon, and spending half your days in a dream, then you are a fool and will be rewarded with a fool's life. You will live in squalor, will always be short of cash, and your children will laugh at you. Accept your fate: don't try a late run. If you do, you will be shot before you finish the first lap.

If *Boss* is your fate, it will appear when you're young. **Truth: If you are a boss in your gray, you were a boss in your green.** Your old age will show a trend line in which you rise above your peers at every stage. When you were a bambino, and the nippers around you were finding ways to turn a dollar, were you pocketing two? Did the

Mustache Petes take a shine to you, making you their errand boy? When the soldiers were squirreling away $100's, were you keeping $1,000's? If so, *Boss* was your fate long before you were a boss. The Family will respect your authority.

RULE

31

CONTROL THE PURSE

With the money of the Church and of his subjects he was able to maintain his armies.

—Niccolò Machiavelli, *The Prince*, 1513

RULE 31:
CONTROL THE PURSE
The boss sends the envelope.

I too wanted to make money, but it would be in my own fashion.

—Joe Bonanno

A boss without cash is vulnerable. Everything around us is measured in decimals; from associate to administration, from poverty to high society, we jump to our feet if a dollar is to be gained. Everyone, whether boss or soldier, is moved by coin.

Truth: He who controls the purse wears the crown. The soldier waiting for the boss to make payroll is dependent: if his cash is slow in coming, he will have trouble paying off the mortgage and the Buick. As boss, then, be the arbiter of the purse. Without bank you are not the boss. You may seem to be, as Fat Tony Salerno did in the Genovese family; but Salerno was a front man, taking the risk for Vincent "Chin" Gigante but reaping no reward. The man who pays you is your boss. When the law knocks, threatening a 100-year sentence, the boss will go free and you will be the fall guy.

Don't be fooled by title or rank. Soldiers and caporegimes may fully obey you, but if you don't control the purse, you are not the boss. Your position is a farce, and once you have outlived your usefulness and nothing more can be gained from you, you will be expelled from the Family and the organization that you have built will call for your execution.

RULE

32

BOSSES TALK
TO BOSSES

The first opinion which one forms of a prince, and of his understanding, is by observing the men he has around him.

—Niccolò Machiavelli, *The Prince*, 1513

RULE 32:
BOSSES TALK TO BOSSES

*I had the feeling of real power. It's what I had always dreamed about, that
someday the biggest people in New York would come up to me to say hello.*

—Charlie "Lucky" Luciano

Bosses keep company with bosses. Once you have risen to *Boss*, don't
make soldiers your friends—leave them to their peers. Wherever you
go, if you find the place full of soldiers, go somewhere else. Truth: a
soldier is poor, so he cannot lend; his rank is low, so he cannot promote;
and his ambitions are humble, so he cannot inspire. His life is struggle,
and if he moves two steps forward he often falls three steps back. **Truth:
A soldier who has no racket has no value.** And in Cosa Nostra, what
has no value does not deserve to live. Under your leadership, the weak
soldier should meet his fate. Avoid such company or risk the dangers
that await it.

As boss, spend your time with men of respect. Once you lead the Family,
talking with the bosses, issuing orders to the caporegimes, and voting
on the Commission, stop exposing yourself to the muck of the rackets.
Truth: The soldier is a beggar; leave him to beg. He will implore
you for advice and favors; ignore him. If he fumes, let him. Take the
piece he owes you and shoo him away, for what value can he bring?
Can he make you capo di tutti capi? Can he advance your plans with the
Commission? Can he cut you in on a piece of the Copacabana? Can he
open up gambling in Havana or Las Vegas and launder dollars for the
president of Cuba? None of the above. So his cries should fall on deaf

ears. Ban him from your administration. Keep him far from everything you do. Send him to work and pay him no mind.

As boss, deal with bosses. If you head the Luciano Family, your conversations should be with the bosses of the Bonanno, Mangano, Profaci, and Gagliano Families. Would a soldier have attended the Apalachin meeting? His words would have drowned serious talk.

For every grievance that the soldier spouts, you, the boss, have had ten. Where the soldier has faltered, you have persevered. That's why you are a boss and the soldier is a soldier. You were a rum runner, a narcotics dealer, a cargo hijacker. You have a scarred face and a lazy eye. You walk with a limp and lack a forefinger and thumb. You have done your service to the street. For all this, you have earned your seat among godfathers in the Honored Society.

In all of your dealings, whether major or trivial, keep company with bosses. The underachieving are not worth your time. A man who has yet to find success for himself will not find it for you. **Truth: Failure invites failure.** No one becomes boss by chance. If you are the boss, you have earned it with bloody knuckles and sacrifice. You have felt the recoil of the revolver and the burn of its heat. You now have the right to lounge in plush property with your friends—your fellow bosses.

RULE

33

DO A FAVOR
FOR A FAVOR

If he whom you help conquers, he remains in your power.

—Niccolò Machiavelli, *The Prince*, 1513

RULE 33:
DO A FAVOR FOR A FAVOR

I brought you up here to do you a favor. Naturally, being a politician, I expect to get a favor in return.

—New York Governor Al Smith to Charlie "Lucky" Luciano

As boss, your power depends on partnership with the affluent and the connected. The most senior of all bosses, the capo di tutti capi, will see his power fade if he lacks the backing of the legislature and the judiciary.

A statesman may not need cash, for his coffers are flush with campaign funds and he has inherited millions. But to win office he needs "every one of those delegates" in Manhattan, Brooklyn, and the Bronx, as New York Governor Al Smith told Lucky Luciano and Frank Costello. He needs Tammany Hall—and you, the boss, pull the levers of Tammany Hall. So when he asks you for a favor, oblige him—but let him know that you too need favors, for your rackets require legislative protections. Repeal of the Volstead Act (which, in 1919, introduced Prohibition, a national ban on alcohol) will damage your Family's bootlegging interests. Offer a trade: the delegates' votes for the statesman's promise to protect the Volstead Act. Otherwise Prohibition will end.

To be owed a favor, you must first have done a favor. **Truth: "To get something you have to give something,"** as John Gotti said. So, as boss, you strengthen yourself where you are weak by bartering your strengths. The cop is badly paid, he needs capital; you—the boss— need your loanshark racket to run uninterrupted, for you make more when you keep the money moving at all times. So you pay off the cop. Your racket will now run without interference.

You are the boss. There is always someone plotting against you, someone who wants to see a sawed-off blowing off your head. Try as you may, if you are the boss, nothing will bring you love; love is displaced by envy. So if you are head of the Family, make sure that you are owed favors. If you are owed twenty favors, you are more protected than if you are owed ten. The judge, the mayor, the banker, the broker, the lawyer, the cop, the Commission, the union local, and the longshoreman, not to mention the pimp, the madam, the bellhop, and the maître d'—they all should owe you favors. Because the day will come when you will need one.

RULE
34

LIVE MODESTLY

It is wiser to put up with the name of being miserly, which breeds ignominy but without hate, than to be obliged, from the desire to be reckoned liberal, to incur the reproach of rapacity which breeds hate as well as ignominy.

—Niccolò Machiavelli, *The Prince*, 1513

RULE 34:
LIVE MODESTLY
Keep a low profile.

I got no big needs. I ain't got no big mansion needs.

—New York Governor Al Smith to Charlie "Lucky" Luciano

Truth: A boss should not make a purchase when he cannot explain how he paid for it.

Truth: The greediest pig in the sty will be first to be led to the slaughterhouse, for its excess fat will produce a succulent capocollo.

So keep your wealth quiet. If it is public, you will become a target. Estes Kefauver will subpoena you to appear before the US Senate's Committee on Organized Crime, which will quiz you on how you came by your riches. If you can't prove your income is legitimate, you'll be marked down as a racketeer.

If you have something to hide, on the witness stand you may sweat, stutter, and suffer "dancing hands," as the press wrote of Frank Costello. Fidgety fingers under questioning will betray your guilt. And even though you're paying "a grease of over a hundred grand a week—ten thousand a week, every week, like clockwork, to the top brass of the Police Department," as Lucky Luciano said he did, it won't help you in the box: public, media, and law will think, "Why is Costello so nervous if he has nothing to hide?" Your partners will worry that they will be looked at too; the police who take your bribes will wonder whether to keep working with you.

And to top it off, you will face increased scrutiny from investigators at the moment when you're the least protected.

So show no sign of wealth that you cannot account for. Since unexplained wealth piques interest, don't wallow in it. Park your valuables out of sight and your dollars in Switzerland. Keep them in America and the state will seize them. **Truth: The American government cannot be trusted, for the government is the people and we-the-people are corrupt.**

A wise boss lives modestly. The Waldorf Astoria has prestige, but its high towers and marble finishes raise the question of how you pay for it. Carlo Gambino and John Gotti declined the Waldorf and lived in row homes in Brooklyn and Queens.

If 100 people know what you have, you have 100 worries. Don't think your wealth brings you friends; it brings you enemies, two for every dollar you own. **Truth: A boss ought not to be "a performance for the media,"** as Sammy "The Bull" Gravano described John Gotti. As boss, you wake daily to people who envy you; don't give them something to see. Your riches can take you around the world—let them take you to Sicily. You have the power to elect governments, you are rich in both cash and influence, you are respectable—what more do you need? Why broadcast your wealth? Big Paul Castellano died by the gun, his body riddled with bullets and a hole in his head—at the behest of a loyalist. **Truth: Big Paul lived in excess.**

RULE
35

BE INFORMED

A Prince should read histories, and in these should note the actions of great men, observe how they conducted themselves in their wars, and examine the causes of their victories and defeats.... A wise prince... should pursue such methods as these, never resting idle in times of peace, but strenuously seeking to turn them to account, so that he may derive strength from them in the hour of danger.

—Niccolò Machiavelli, *The Prince*, 1513

RULE 35:
BE INFORMED
Keep abreast of the world around you.

Meyer Lansky was always reading, always learning something mostly having to do with numbers. That's when I started reading.

—Charlie "Lucky" Luciano

For a boss, worldly knowledge is good. If you don't know local politics, how will you buy the mayor and the governor? How will you know the price of a delegate or a jury member? Don't be the boss who offers five when the cost is ten, who offers politicians cash when they need votes. Fill your mental bank with the state's business, and when the opportunity arises, propose solutions to its problems. The state will protect you in return.

If you, the boss, own delegates and their votes, you have the power Lucky Luciano had to look Al Smith in the eye and "give it to him straight: 'What the hell are you doing, governor? You're trying to repeal Prohibition, and that's going to throw us all out of business.'" The governor will offer trade: "I intend to get that nomination and I intend to win this election. Line up overwhelming support for me from Manhattan, Brooklyn and the Bronx, where you fellows control the delegates. I want every one of those delegates at the convention in Houston. If I get them, I'm prepared to make things good for you."

As boss, brief yourself in all matters of interest to your world. At the local, state, and federal level, be informed. When the governor announces his run for the presidency, you should know in advance and be ready with payola. When communism takes over Cuba and shuts down your rackets there, you should be prepared with casinos in Las Vegas. When a New York journalist, Carlo Tresca, criticizes Benito Mussolini, you should know. Now you can offer Mussolini service and order Tresca killed, having him shot in the back of the head, as Vito Genovese did. In matters both domestic and foreign, a boss must have his finger on the pulse of global affairs.

Whether you get the news televised or in a newspaper at your door in the morning, you should take it in. When Lucky Luciano was sitting in Dannemora during World War II, he read the daily news about the Axis occupation of Sicily. So informed, he was able to strategize his way out of prison by providing US Naval Intelligence with information and with Sicilian contacts who could be trusted to assist the Allied invasion of the island. His contribution to the war effort got him out of prison.

So don't start your day until you're up to date. At night, study. Sugar Ray might be fighting Jake LaMotta, but nothing should rob your books and your sources of your attention. The soldier spends his time on clubbing and girls. He wastes his money on whores and coke. Then he feels sorry for himself. **Truth: The soldier is short of options because he is short of knowledge.** Old or young, study history, current events, the social climate, mathematics, and the teachings of Niccolò Machiavelli. Do this and your options are limitless.

RULE
36

BUY A PLOT

As they had found him a most valiant and skilful leader when, under his command, they defeated the Duke of Milan, and, on the other hand, saw him slack in carrying on the war, they made up their minds that no further victories were to be had under him; and because, through fear of losing what they had gained, they neither could nor would discharge him, to secure themselves against him they were forced to put him to death.

—Niccolò Machiavelli, *The Prince*, 1513

RULE 36:
BUY A PLOT
Every boss has his day.

In this secret society, there's one way in and there's only one way out. You come in on your feet and you go out in a coffin.

—Paul Castellano

You are the boss. You built the distilleries, cut the scotch and the bourbon, sourced the offshore connections, paid the rum-runners, financed the speedboats. You are New York's biggest bootlegger. Every speak and brothel offers King's Ransom Scotch, the finest on the market, and you part-own the company.

You have made yourself a millionaire, respected by the bankers and the businessmen. You live in the Majestic and in a mansion on Long Island. You have shares in the Beverly Club and the Copacabana. Your gambling interests turn seven-figure profits. Long ago, as a whippersnapper, you promised your mama that you would amount to something, and you do. Your cars are luxury and your suits are tailored. You have a wife who is costly and a mistress who is more so. You own politicians, union locals, cops. A wiretap recorded a judge in New York's highest court promising you loyalty. You have the millions and the minions, both acquired by trickery. You have frolicked with Dean Martin and Frank Sinatra. You have laid beautiful women, driven Cadillacs, eaten the finest cuisine. With your millions safe in Swiss banks, you sleep sound, knowing that your nest egg is secure and your gray years will be plush. **Truth: As boss, you have it all. If life is a mountain, you have reached its peak.**

But every boss must fall from the mountain he has scaled.

Have you corrupted governments, local, national, and international? Have you gouged the public, inflating their cost of living by making the businesses they shop at pay the *pizzo*, the extortion fee? Has your greed left the poor worse off? Have you charged $50 for what should cost $25? Have you opened speaks and brothels, and sold narcotics, in poor neighborhoods, contributing to their ruin? **Truth: Of all this you are guilty.**

Truth: You, the boss, are "a big fat bundle of shit." You "look like a pig on two legs." Your Family is a "fucked-up operation," you are "nothing better than a big tub of horseshit," and you will soon "stop being a pig and become a corpse"—all this as Lucky Luciano described "Joe the Boss" Masseria. But Lucky was no better: his decades of robbing the public made him, too, a pig on two legs—him and every other boss. The earth is for the nurturing and protection of the poor, the common, the giving; a boss instead despoils it.

As boss, you thought your millions would protect you. **Truth: For the scum that you are and the devastation you have caused, pain will come.** Your downfall will be televised for your public. Those who once feared you will taunt you. The weak will test and best you. The soldier who once kissed your ring will decide your fate. The bullet will pierce your skin, and if you survive the bullet you will die instead by jury: the prison gate will ring in your ear, with a sentence of a century. **Truth: It is more honorable to die by the gun.** So when your time arrives, be dignified: look into your assassin's eyes and say, as Bonanno caporegime Sonny Black did, "Hit me one more time and make it good."

The rose is beautiful, but it sprouts thorns as well as petals and in time it withers away. The cold must come and the frost must bite. **Truth: You, the boss, have brought smiles as a rose does, but your thorns have also drawn blood, and in time you will die as the rose will.** So, on your first day as boss, buy a burial plot and commission a marble tomb. On its top, have your name carved in bold letters, ensuring that it will live on, as a boss's name should. *So long, pal.*

I acknowledge all enemies of systems and conformity.
To all who have died to that end and to all who risk death to do it —
I, RJ Roger, acknowledge you. You are the real Bosses.

To David Frankel: Thank you for being a friend to my book.
You have taught me the value of an editor.

To Joost Elffers: Thank you for believing; for fighting until the end.
Through agreement and disagreement; good days and bad,
together we crossed the finish line. It has been my honor
to work alongside your brilliance.